Parenting Boys

How to Deal With Misbehaving and Challenging Toddlers

(Nurturing Your Boy's Development in Each Stage From an Infant to a Young Adult)

James Hinderliter

Published by Rob Miles

© **James Hinderliter**

All Rights Reserved

Parenting Boys: How to Deal With Misbehaving and Challenging Toddlers (Nurturing Your Boy's Development in Each Stage From an Infant to a Young Adult)

ISBN 9781990084355

All rights reserved. No part of this guide may be reproduced in any form without permission in writing from the publisher except in the case of brief quotations embodied in critical articles or reviews.

Legal & Disclaimer

The information contained in this book is not designed to replace or take the place of any form of medicine or professional medical advice. The information in this book has been provided for educational and entertainment purposes only.

The information contained in this book has been compiled from sources deemed reliable, and it is accurate to the best of the Author's knowledge; however, the Author cannot guarantee its accuracy and validity and cannot be held liable for any errors or omissions. Changes are periodically made to this book. You must consult your doctor or get professional medical advice before using any of the suggested remedies, techniques, or information in this book.

Upon using the information contained in this book, you agree to hold harmless the Author from and against any damages, costs, and expenses, including any legal fees potentially resulting from the application of any of the information provided by this guide. This disclaimer applies to any damages or injury caused by the use and application, whether directly or indirectly, of any advice or information presented, whether for breach of contract, tort, negligence, personal injury, criminal intent, or under any other cause of action.

You agree to accept all risks of using the information presented inside this book. You need to consult a professional medical practitioner in order to ensure you are both able and healthy enough to participate in this program.

Table of Contents

INTRODUCTION 1

CHAPTER 1: BECOMING A STEP PARENT 4

CHAPTER 2: PARENTING 101–ON DISCIPLINING TECHNIQUES 13

CHAPTER 3: TALK TO YOUR CHILDREN 25

CHAPTER 4: HANDLING KIDS 32

CHAPTER 5: LESSON ON ENCOURAGING EXPLORATION AND DEVELOPING CURIOSITY 45

CHAPTER 6: SOME MORE TIPS FOR PARENTS OF CHILDREN WITH STRONG CHARACTERS 49

CHAPTER 7: HOW TO FOSTER IDENTITY 53

CHAPTER 8: GETTING ALONG WITH YOUR TEENS 68

CHAPTER 9: HOW DO I DEAL WITH MY TEENAGER'S FLUCTUATING MOODS? 73

CHAPTER 10: YOUR CHILD'S TRAINING AND DISCIPLINE .. 78

CHAPTER 11: GENERAL HEALTH 96

CHAPTER 12: BEHAVIOURAL PROBLEMS 110

CHAPTER 13: SINGLE MOM - REWARDS FOR GOOD BEHAVIOR KIDS WILL LOVE 121

CHAPTER 14: DISCIPLINE 128

CHAPTER 15: DISCIPLINE STRATEGIES FOR TODDLERS ... 132

CHAPTER 16: MORE TIPS IN RAISING YOUR DAUGHTER WELL 144

CHAPTER 17: LIFE AHEAD FOR A CONFIDENT GIRL 150

CHAPTER 18: MODERN CHILDREN AND RELIGION 154

CHAPTER 19: COPING WITH LONG-DISTANCE PARENTING 159

CHAPTER 20: GIVE THEM TIME 175

CHAPTER 21: WHERE THE BABY SHOULD SLEEP AND EAT IN AN RV 182

CHAPTER 22: FRIENDS & SIBLINGS 188

CONCLUSION 194

Introduction

This book contains timely information, tips, and advice on single fatherhood meant to help single dads who for one reason or another are suddenly faced with the responsibility of raising their children all by themselves.

With statistics showing more and more fathers becoming single dads at an ever increasing rate, it is not surprising to see a great number of them desperately seeking help on how to face the challenges of single fatherhood. Fathers have always played a rather limited role in raising their young children – providing for and protecting their families. It has always been the moms who shoulder the bulk of the responsibilities and sacrifice a great deal of their time rearing the kids.

Taking over the role of moms without neglecting their dad roles can be a seemingly insurmountable task for the suddenly single dads. It is tough enough for two parents to raise their young children, and tougher even for single moms to raise theirs, how much more for single dads who by force of circumstances have to assume both sets of responsibilities at the same time – role playing for the first time mommy tasks they have long taken for granted or were never even aware of?

Certainly single dads need all the help they can get especially since they will have to face much more difficult and unique parenting challenges than single moms. For example, single dads have to help their children cope with not having their moms (whom they have been attached to and identified with since birth) around when they need them. Another ticklish situation for single dads is having girls to raise girls through their puberty and teens. While this may not be a problem for single moms since they have gone through the same stage before, for single dads, it will be truly challenging and difficult and may even require getting help from outside.

This book addresses all these major single fatherhood concerns plus a host of other challenging tasks single dads need to hurdle while raising their young children alone. It contains a treasure trove of single parenting tips and ideas that will help single dads overcome the many challenges that will confront them along the way.

Tackling the many challenges associated with raising the young children head on will not only be easy but will also be enjoyable for single dads if done properly – especially so if you have a network of friends and family to support you. Put in a lot of love, patience, and perseverance, plus a lot of help from your support community and single fatherhood will be truly fulfilling.

Chapter 1: Becoming A Step Parent

Turning into a parent by mixing families or wedding somebody with children can be a remunerating and satisfying experience. If you have never had children, you will get the chance to impart your life to a more youthful individual and shape his or her character. If you have children, you will offer them more chances to strengthen relationships and build up a unique bond that no one but kin can have.

Your new relatives may get along effortlessly, however, on many occasions you can expect problems along the way. Making sense of your role as a parent likewise may prompt disarray or even clash between yourself and your partner, your partner's ex wife, or ex-husband and their children.

While there is no fail-safe equation for making the perfect family, it is imperative to approach this new circumstance with persistence and comprehension for the sentiments of those included. Here is the way to make things less demanding as you adjust to your new role.

Begin gradually

The underlying role of a step parent is that of another affectionate grown-up in a kid's life, like an adoring relative or a tutor. You may fancy a closer bond immediately and might ponder what you are doing incorrectly if your new step child does not warm up to you or your children as fast as you would like, however, connections need time to develop.

Begin to ease back and do whatever it takes not to hurry into things. Give things a chance to grow actually, children can tell if grown-ups are being fake or undependable.

After some time, you can build up a more profound, more significant association with your step children, which does not need to look like the one they impart to their biological parents.

Factors that affect your relationship

Kids who are grieving the passing of an expired parent or the detachment or separation of their biological parents may require time to adjust themselves before they can completely acknowledge you as a step parent.

For those whose biological parents are still alive, remarriage may mean the end of trust that their folks will rejoin. Regardless of the fact that it has been quite a long while since the detachment, kids (even adolescents/teens) frequently cling to that expectation for quite a while. From the children's point of view, this reality can make them feel furious, hurt, and befuddled.

The following may influence the move into step parenting:

☐ Age of the children. With regards to altering and shaping new relationships, smaller children for the most part have a less demanding time than grown-up children.

☐ Duration of your acquaintance. As a rule, the more you know the children, the better the relationship. There are special cases, yet by and large having a history together makes the move a little smoother.

☐ Length of time you have been in touch with the parent before marriage. Once more, there are special cases, however, ordinarily in the event that you do not hurry into the association with the grown-up, children have a decent sense that you are in this for the long-run.

☐ Duration the parent you wed coexists with the ex-life partner. This is a basic element. Insignificant clash and open correspondence between ex-husband or ex-wife can have a major impact with respect to how effortlessly kids acknowledge you as their step parent. It is much less taxing for children to move to new living arrangements when grown-ups keep negative remarks out of earshot.

☐ Extent of time you spend with children. Attempting to bond with children each weekend can be a troublesome approach to make companions with your new step kids. Keep in mind to put their requirements first. If kids need time with their biological parents, they ought to get it. So making yourself rare can smooth the way to a superior relationship over the long-run.

Knowing early what circumstances may get to be hazardous as you unite new relatives can help you plan so that, if inconveniences emerge, you can deal with them with an additional dosage of persistence and poise.

Ventures to admirable step parenting

All parents face challenges every so often. In any case, when you are a step parent, those snags are intensified by the way that you are not the biological parent; this can open up force battles inside the family, whether it is from the children, your partner's ex, or even your partner.

When things get difficult putting children's needs first can help you use sound judgment. Here's the way:

☐Put needs, not wants, first. Kids need adoration, warmth, and predictable principles most importantly. Giving them toys or treats, particularly if they are not in relation to good behavior or otherwise can give rise to a situation where you have an inclination that you are exchanging presents for affection. Also, in the event that you feel regretful for treating your biological children uniquely in contrast to your step children, do not dole out freebies to compensate for it. Do your best to make sense of how to treat them all the more similarly.

☐House rules matter. Keep your home principles as reliable as could reasonably be expected for all children, whether they are your children from a past relationship, your partner's children from a past relationship, or new kids you have had together. Kids and adolescents will have distinctive standards, however, they ought to be reliably connected at all times.

This assist kids acclimate to moves, such as moving to another house or greeting a new born, and helps them feel that all children in your house are dealt with similarly. In the event that children are managing two altogether different arrangements of guidelines in every home, it might be the ideal opportunity for a grown-ups family meeting; generally children can figure out how to work the system for their benefit in the short-run as against long-run issues.

☐ Create new family customs. Discover uncommon activities to do with your step kids, however, make sure to get their criticism. Some new family conventions could incorporate board game nights, bicycle riding together, cooking, art and craft, or even playing word games in the automobile. The key is to have a fabulous time together, not to attempt to win their adoration; children are savvy and will rapidly make sense of in case you are attempting to constrain a relationship.

☐ Respect all parents. At the point when a partner's ex is deceased, it is vital to be delicate to and respect that individual. In the event that yourself and your partner share custody with the biological parent, attempt to be considerate and humane in your cooperation with each other. Never say negative things in regards to biological parent before the children. Doing as such regularly angers the children with the parent making the comments. No youngster likes to hear their folks reprimanded, regardless of the possibility that he or she is grumbling about them to you.

☐ Do not utilize kids as envoys or go-betweens. Do whatever it takes not to question kids about what is occurring in the other family unit; they will disdain it when they feel that they are being requested to spy on another parent. Wherever conceivable, discuss straightforwardly with the other parent about important matters, for example, planning, appearance, well-being issues, or school issues. Online guardianship timetables make this procedure somewhat less demanding in light of the fact that parents can note appearance days and offer this data with each other through the Internet.

☐ Talk to your partner or companion. Correspondence between yourself and your partner is essential so you can settle on child rearing choices together. This is particularly pivotal in the event that you each have distinctive thoughts on child rearing and discipline. In case you are new to child rearing as a step parent, ask your partner what might be the most ideal approach to become acquainted with the children. Use assets to discover what children of various ages are occupied with and keep in mind to ask them.

Chapter 2: Parenting 101–On Disciplining Techniques

There must be confidence in parenting. Confidence is what makes parents positive, in charge, and effective. Notice that when your confidence level is high, the daily hassles of living and dealing with challenging toddlers become an easy feat. But when your confidence crumbles, just like parents experience most of the time, you will quickly lose all the right perspective that you have set and that easy feat, walk in the park day suddenly becomes one messy and extra exhausting day.

Confidence has an effect in everything that you do. For parents, confidence brings forth effective discipline, which ultimately improves your child's behavior and builds his own self-confidence as well. But just how confident are you in parenting your children? Are you the type who is 50-50?

Are you unsure if what you are doing is right? It may be a bit strange that despite self-help books, how-to manuals, and child care professionals, parents still feel short when it comes to parenting. You need to appear sure in your decisions even if you are not. If you've ever been travelling and a car and two people tell you different directions. Who is the one you usually go with? The majority of the time it's the person who is most sure in what they are saying. This is a certainty bias which means we are more likely to believe and follow people who are certain in what they are doing. Your child needs to know that you know what you are doing. They are reliant on you, so make sure you back up your decisions with confidence.

Yes, life has become tough for parents today because of many different factors such as becoming overwhelmed with information, isolation, lifestyle, competition, and many more. What is important is that you are confident that you are doing a great job, although most parents fail to realize this. The fact that you are lovingly attending to your toddler's every need, waking up in the middle of the night to change his nappies or feed him – these are all good reasons to worry about how you parent your child.

Remember, parenting is a compromise. We start with high ideals but later on lower the sights simply because you are human, and you become tired and exhausted. It is not for you to compare. What feels right and works for you is as good a way to bring up your children as any other parents do. Just keep in mind that if you love your kids, you must enjoy them. Do what feels right and learn to slow down. Not soon enough, you will find yourselves with kids no longer expressing the needs to have their parents around. So for as long as they need you, be there, and give the best you've got.

How to Discipline A Child in A Way That doesn't Affect Their Self Esteem Later in Life

What we say to our kids has a profound effect on their self-image. Words that come out when we're in a highly emotional state could define their lives. Children grow up thinking they're bad and attach their identity to be that person, and it leads to a whole road of trouble. What we say can have a massive effect on the child's self-esteem. We want our children to have every advantage they can in life and it's our responsibility to help ensure this. According to leading self-esteem expert Nathaniel Branden the best way to punish a child for a wrong they have committed is the following: Condemn the action and not the child. This means tell the child, what they have done is bad instead of, the child themselves being bad. By doing this, you teach the child a sense of morality without causing them to form an identity to a specific action. Think about it, you are their main authority in life. You teach them the majority of the things they know, if you tell them that they are bad, enough times at an impressionable age, they'll start to believe you and develop an identity around it. It can be a major hindrance to self-esteem which is something everyone deserves. So condemn the action and not the child.

Techniques of Discipline

If there is one thing parents need to know when it comes to parenting, it is the fact that is not all about punishment. Discipline is about encouraging, shaping, and rewarding your toddler to behave in the correct way. Discipline should be something positive rather than the nasty, negative stuff.

So what is the best way?

First, you need to start with the tone of voice. A parent should learn how to say encouraging words such as "Good job", "You did well", "You are so good", Well done" – all these coupled with the way you look at your toddler when you say it and how you hold him will all make a big difference. What is important is that you learn how to transmit that love through your eyes and words. Think about this, one of the main goals for your toddler is to get your attention. If they get more attention by misbehaving than doing something good, they'll misbehave. It wouldn't make sense for them to go for the option that provides less attention. So really play up the fact when they do something good.

These kinds of tones and actions should be mainly used in disciplining your toddler. When they are not behaving the way you would want them to be, you again transmit your message with your voice, only this time firmer, more serious, and with a tone of disapproval. You don't have to shout just to send your message across. If you are shouting, they will realize it's a more effective way to get your attention. They may not understand the whole thing, but at least they know that you are not pleased with the behavior.

The following are tips on how to discipline your challenging toddler without resorting to that old smacking or "go to your room" method.

Know what winds up your toddler – you probably know by now what makes your child misbehave and what makes them and the rest of the household have a terrible day. Knowing the trigger before it becomes a full blown, hard to control one. The best confrontation is one that doesn't happen. If it can be prevented. Sometimes it will necessary to show your child if something is or isn't acceptable however other times it can be avoided if you know what sets them off.

Take, for example, bringing your child to supermarkets or in the cinemas. Some parents would question why their toddler misbehaves at these places while other children do not. What they do not know is that there are those parents who never really bring their children to supermarkets and cinemas because they will know what will happen and they know exactly how their children would behave in such places. And so, they intentionally avoid these places. So if you know that bringing your toddler to a supermarket will only make them throw tantrums, and you can avoid bringing them, do not bring them. It is as simple as that. You should also keep in mind it is best to take your toddler shopping at a time when they are not tired. It can be a big emotional drain on them doing this, so try to take them at a time where they are alert to decrease the chances of a tantrum.

They want your undivided attention – Admit it or not, attention is sometimes only partly given to children. This is because most parents are busy with chores and other pressing matters and errands. Giving your undivided attention to your toddler is perhaps the greatest reward you will ever give them. Sadly, this does not happen all the time.

If you find it hard to do so, make sure you make up for the lost time. Make your children your priority above all other things. Yes, there may be immediate concerns to attend to, but you must find ways to do both without compromising your time and attention with them. Remember, they rely on you and you alone, so give them what is most needed.

Focus on what really matters — simply put, do not get drawn with the idea of having a bad day because a child misbehaves. Avoid complaining about irrelevant stuff or get so stirred up with how your child behaves. Most of all, do not ever compare your toddler to other toddlers. The trick here is to focus on what matters even if it is hard to do so. Did you know that selective deafness works sometimes? When your child shouts, "I love you, Dad", reply with "I love You too, son". But when he shouts "I hate you, Daddy!", do not get so stirred up that you will shout "I hate you, too!" back. When you are at the edge of losing your patience, know that it will get you nowhere if you will just get mad. The effects of saying such things to a child could have serious long term implications so always remember the bigger picture.

Stop looking for logic – because chances are, you won't find any. There is no point in saying your child exists to annoy you for the rest of your life or ruin your once serene life. Why? Because your toddler does not know what they are doing and is definitely not doing anything of the sort. Your toddler is just being a toddler. That is it. They have a very short attention span and punishing him for disobeying you or locking him in his room will not solve the issue. A logical debate with them is a waste of time. Leave it until they come of age.

There must be clear communication – Positive and confident parenting is most effective if you know how to communicate well with your child. Be firm with your rules and let him know when you are upset or about to get upset. Teach him that when mommy says it is time to pick up your mess, now is the time and it must be done. But of course, you do not expect them to obey at once. If this happens, say something like, "Honey, I'll give you a hand I n picking those toys. Let's both pick those up and put them in the toy box. Help me, okay?" If you start doing things like this. It is a win/win for both of you. They get to spend time with you and you help achieve the task. Start thinking in win/wins

Divert their attention – this is considered one of the most effective ways to disciplining toddlers. We all know that they are easily diverted. So when your toddler is about to touch an electric cord or that fancy dress of yours, you can try diverting his attention by saying something like this "Hey, look birds!" Or, "Oh, there are dogs outside, let's go have a look." This often works. You may be lying there for a second, but this could save everybody including your sanity.

Chapter 3: Talk To Your Children

Millions of children of several age ranges, perhaps basically teenagers, do continuously share their complaints about not having effective and active communication with their parents, who in turn do not even know a thing about their children, their needs and wants, their problems and daily events, their personal lives and even their personal interests and hobbies. This lack of communication is attributed to a number of reasons, mentioning some as follows:

Parents being too busy in their personal affairs to turn an eye to what is happening with their children.

Parents may be not that busy – they actually do have time for their children yet are unable to seize it properly or communicate skilfully.

It happens in so many cases that the parents are quite bad in communicating;

bad to a gruesome extent that is manifested by aggressing their children, continuously scolding and scorning them, shouting at them with and without a clear reason, sometimes beating them up, also with and without a clear reason. These actions have caused a lot of children to become retracted from their parents and not wishing any longer to connect with them out of fear and terror.

Let's imagine how pleasant it feels when you approach your child as a little friend of yours. While you are entitled to create boundaries with which you can supervise and monitor your child's activity, it is also highly recommended to establish a very firm bridge that represents the means of communication between you both. Here are some tips and facts regarding talking to your kid:

With a kind and encouraging tone, approach your child with questions about their hobbies, interests, how their school day was, what they would like to eat and so forth. Through talking, make your child feel you are interested in what they do and what they like. Talking to your child opens up a chance for you to share not only conversations but also memories and moments. The more you talk to your kid friendly and lovingly, the more you show curiosity and care towards what's on their minds, the more moments and more time you would get to share together. Introduce conversations with your kid regarding where they would like to go, what they would like to play or practise. Show them your interest in taking part with them and encourage them to speak up about the things they like and wish to do, no matter how simple and perhaps "superficial" they are. This would definitely contribute to reinforcing communication bridges between you both and brings your child closer and closer to you, boosting up their confidence and willingness to share anything off the top of their head with you without feeling embarrassed or too shy. On the other hand, talk to your kid when you want to do something particular, for example read a book, watch a film or go for a walk. Initiate the conversation and invite them for sharing the activity with you. It is recommended for you to initiate it firstly as your child may be too shy and/or hesitant to do so out of their own will. Later on, your child would become more confident in that remit and more motivated to approach you and suggest doing things together. This is also a very important part of developing parent-child connections, and contributes to developing a fruitful and healthy relationship in the future that can be considered a lovely blend of parenting and friendship. It is highly favourable and recommended for everyone to have parents as the first best friends, and here comes the important role of the parents in accomplishing that. Having parents as best friends empowers the child throughout their life, knowing that no matter what they encounter in their daily life and how severe and intolerable things can become around them, there is always that refuge which they can seek any time, in which exist those who are ready to be here for them all the time, unconditionally and wholeheartedly.

When you allow an opportunity for your child to interact with you honestly about what they want and think about, they would approach you every time with comfort, security and confidence in themselves and in you. When you show empathy, interest, patience and tolerance, care and serenity towards what they say, they would be encouraged to become an open book to you and share so many things with you no matter how superficial or serious they are. They would not be too concerned of you reacting negatively to them. Embracing your child with positive emotions and interactions would efficiently driving them away from hiding things from you and/or lying. Children usually tend to hide and/or lie basically out of fear of how their parents would react: yelling at them, beating them up, grounding them, etc... This indeed brings nothing but unfavourable outcomes, cracks the bond between the child and parents, renders it more and more fragile, and may eventually lead to complete estrangement from each other. It is ultimately and inevitably important to have your child, especially at their early life stage and their teens, telling you everything and opening up to you. It matters a lot when you provide them the chance of doing so with comfort and relief, and without any fear of you punishing them and/or reacting against them while they are awaiting your support. In this regard, you ought to remember that you are expected to support your child even when they are wrong. It entails some intelligence on your end but can be fulfilled. When your child makes a mistake and approaches you with trust in you, guide them towards what it correct, explain the mistake and why it is considered a mistake. Sometimes it deserves some yelling at them, go for it if needed (but not too much! Modifying your tone to become strict and firm can do good, no need to shout and scare the world out of your kid!) – encourage them to behave better in the next times. Blame them for their dereliction if they manifest any, but do not disappoint them and destroy their optimism about you being supportive of them. The act is support is not only for doing the right thing; it is manifested as well in the form of constructive criticism and guidance that is oriented towards improving the child and securing their advantage.

Chapter 4: Handling Kids

Strategies and Solutions for Handling a Difficult Child

What is the best way to handle a "difficult" child?

Here are some general strategies and solutions to help you live with a youngster with bothersome temperament traits:

First, recognize that much of your child's behavior reflects his character.

Establish a neutral or objective emotional climate in which to deal with your child. Try not to respond in an emotional and instinctive manner, which is unproductive.

Don't take your child's behavior personally. Temperament is innate, and your child probably is not purposely trying to be difficult or irritating. Don't blame him or yourself.

Try to prioritize the issues and problems surrounding your child. Some are more important and deserve greater attention. Others are not as relevant and can be either ignored or put "way down the list."

Focus on the issues of the moment. Do not project into the future.

Review your expectations of your child, your preferences and your values. Are they realistic and appropriate? When your youngster does something right, praise him and reinforce the specific behaviors that you like.

Consider your own temperament and behavior, and how they might also be difficult. Think how you might need to adjust yourself a bit to encourage a better fit with your child.

Anticipate impending high-risk situations, and try to avoid or minimize them. Accept the possibility that this may be a difficult day or circumstance, and be prepared to make the best of it.

Find a way to get some relief for yourself and your child by scheduling some time apart.

Seek professional help, when needed, from your pediatrician.

Engagement with child

Piling workloads and tightening work schedules leave parents with very short time to spend with their child. Mounting household chores cut through what little time they might manage to cook up. Even for homemakers, the scene isn't any brighter. So the whole question arises on how to engage children at home all through the day.

Kids, being little balls of curiosity, get bored of the same activity very quickly and are constantly looking for new and new challenges. This often leaves parents clueless as to how to engage a child.

As a result, parents usually turn to the go to solution of today's world – gadgets. These gadgets with their overflowing stream of contents, keep children engaged day-in and out. But are these gadgets the right way to engage children?

No, they aren't!

There's more to engaging children with meaningful activities than just ridding them of their boredom. **Senior Psychologist Gayathri Rao** from YourDOST explains, "Every child needs to have physical activity and cognitively stimulating tasks every day

Engaging children – why it matters!

Proper fostering

How often have you boasted that your child is mimicking you, even at a very young age?

Children are exposed to a lot of different things while growing up and they acquire all that they observe.

Meaningful activities are essential in teaching the right ideals. It not only ensures that your child gets to learn right from wrong, but also builds his/her knowledge base.

Better social interaction

Communication and social interaction are the backbone of a child's development!

Without proper communication, your child will be unable to develop interactive skills which will affect his/her school life and eventually even work life.

But with meaningful activities your child gets engaged, interacts more, and thereby becomes more social.

Improved focus

Focus is essential for everything – from day-to-day activities to leisure-time reading. Lack of concentration affects not just academics, but even performance in small tasks.

By engaging children with meaningful activities — like playing chess, you can easily increase their concentration.

Healthy body

It is a generally known fact that the main aim of early age physical activities is to build a healthy body. So do you think your child gets enough physical activity?

To answer that, just remember how you used to run around and play in your childhood. Is your little one getting the same amount of movement? This is exactly why you need to engage him/her with meaningful activities like walking, running, etc.

Only then will your little one be able to develop stronger bones, muscles, better reflexes, and in turn a better immune system.

Develop imagination

When was the last time you saw your child playing with an imaginary friend? Imagination is key to your child's development.

Only through imagination does your kid get new ideas and try them out in the real world, testing his/her own limits.

Activities like reading, playing, etc. develop imagination and creativity. Apart from that, they also help in developing brain function.

For working parents the overdue tasks and the scheduled appointments never seem to stop. **Gayathri Rao a Senior Psychologist** shares some tips as to how these challenges can be met. She explains,

Avoid bringing work home with you. In case you have to, allow your child to sit with you. Engage them in an activity that would require them to think and concentrate. (A jigsaw puzzle, or coloring etc.) So they don't disturb you, but still get to spend time with you.

When you do have time to spend with your child, do things that they enjoy. Avoid reprimanding them, nor talking about school work/grades, during this time you.

Take them out with you, when you need to run errands. Be it paying bills, giving your vehicle for service or going grocery shopping.

Listen to your child. Even if it's for 5 minutes a day and he/she wants to talk about the bug crawling in the garden, listen. It's better than spending 3 hours with them and you talking all the while.

Always be reachable to your child. Even if you can't take a call or respond immediately, leave a message saying you will call back, and make sure you do.

Likes and dislikes

The year between age 2 and age 3 is an exciting one. Toddlers are realizing that they are separate individuals from their parents and caregivers. This means that they are driven to assert themselves, to communicate their likes and dislikes, and to act independently (as much as they can!). Toddlers are also developing the language skills that help them express their ideas, wants, and needs.

At the same time, toddlers do not understand logic and still have a hard time with waiting and self-control. In a nutshell: Two-year-olds want what they want when they want it. This is why you may be hearing things like "no" and "me do it" and "no diaper change!" more than ever before.

Learning to Handle Strong Feelings

As a parent, your job is to help your young toddler navigate the tide of strong emotions she is experiencing this year. This is no small task, because the emotional lives of 2-year-olds are complex. This year they are beginning to experience feelings like pride, shame, guilt, and embarrassment for the first time.

Older toddlers are a lot like teenagers. Their feelings may swing wildly from moment to moment. They may be joyful when getting a Popsicle and then despair when it drips on their hands. So toddlers really need your loving guidance to figure out how to cope with their

Practicing Self-Control

When you see challenging behaviour, it usually means that your child can't figure out how to express her feelings in an acceptable way or doesn't know how to get a need met. What helps your child learn is when your response shows her a different, more constructive way to handle these feelings.

Learning to cope with strong feelings usually happens naturally as children develop better language skills in their third year and have more experience with peers, handling disappointment, and following rules. Although children won't completely master self-control until they are school-age (and practice it all their lives!), here are some ideas for helping your toddler begin to learn this important skill:

Violence and non-violence

There are two distinct types of violence experienced by children (defined by the United Nations as anyone aged 0-18 years) - child maltreatment by parents and caregivers in children aged 0-14, and violence occurring in community settings among adolescents aged 15-18 years. These different types of violence can be prevented by addressing the underlying causes and risk factors specific to each type.

Child maltreatment by parents and caregivers can be prevented by:

reducing unintended pregnancies;

reducing harmful levels of alcohol and illicit drug use during pregnancy;

reducing harmful levels of alcohol and illicit drug use by new parents;

improving access to high quality pre- and post-natal services;

providing home visitation services by professional nurses and social workers to families where children are at high-risk of maltreatment;

Providing training for parents on child development, non-violent discipline and problem-solving skills.

Violence involving children in community settings can be prevented through:

pre-school enrichment programmers to give young children an educational head start;

life skills training;

assisting high-risk adolescents to complete schooling;

reducing alcohol availability through the enactment and enforcement of liquor licensing laws, taxation and pricing;

Restricting access to firearms.

Improving the efficiency of pre-hospital and emergency medical care will reduce the risk of death, the time for recovery and the level of long-term impairment due to violence.

All violence against children and especially child maltreatment occurring in the first decade of life is both a problem in itself and a major risk factor for other forms of violence and health problems through a person's life

Chapter 5: Lesson On Encouraging Exploration And Developing Curiosity

Children who love learning and discovering new things are more likely to grow up smart, happy, and emotionally strong than those who are not as interested in exploring their surroundings. That said, developing curiosity in your children is one of the best parenting secrets, and one that you should definitely follow. Go through the rest of this chapter for more information.

How Curiosity Helps Kids

There are many benefits to teaching and encouraging kids to be curious about their surroundings. To start, a love for learning will make going to school more enjoyable for children. This is important, as it is common knowledge that a lot of kids treat this as more of a chore that they need to do rather than something that can help them secure a brighter future. This negative attitude towards learning can result in them not being able to realize their full potential later on in life.

Developing your children's curiosity also helps in their development, especially mentally and intellectually. Through observation, they are able to grasp the idea of cause and effect better, which in turn makes it easier for them to understand new concepts. Exploration also makes them smarter in a sense, as it allows them to learn new things.

What You Can Do to Develop Curiosity in Kids

There are many ways by which you can develop your child's curiosity. Here are some of them:

Do physical activities that include the element of discovery. Going hiking or better yet, camping, will not only help in the physical development of your kids – it also encourages them to explore their surroundings.

Play games that encourage thinking and exploration. A great example is the game "I Spy". Kids love this, and you are subtly helping them hone their powers of observation and encouraging exploration. When it comes to thinking games, try teaching them chess and/or Scrabble as soon as possible.

Don't always give your kids the answers to their questions. Readily providing information when it's asked of you will lead to your children being dependent on you for answers. It also makes them lazy, as they do not have to search for the information they need themselves. Thus they are not able to develop their observation skills, and you won't be able to instill in them a love for learning. It is important, then, that you encourage them to look for the answers to their questions instead of providing these yourself.

Make sure that they have free time. Resist the urge to fill your children's schedules with various activities to the point that they do not have time to relax. Otherwise, there's a real risk that the said activities will cease to be enjoyable for them, and it's highly likely that they'll suffer from a burnout. Instead of doing this to expose them to new things, give them some free time: letting them do what they want is a better way to encourage exploration and discovery.

Join them in discovering new things. Parents are the first and best teachers to their kids, so it is important that you find time to explore your surroundings with them. This will not only deepen your bond with them – it also allows you to augment and correct whatever information they are able to glean from their observation of the things around them.

Chapter 6: Some More Tips For Parents Of Children With Strong Characters

The previous chapters will help you solve some of your worst problems with your child. But here are eleven more impactful tips that will revolutionize your relationship with him:

Always bear in mind your child's age. The younger he is, the more he depends on you for guidance and the less he can communicate verbally. He may throw more tantrums because he is frustrated by his inability to communicate.

Be mindful of your child's age relative to his siblings. If he is the eldest, he naturally wants to dominate and command, and you inadvertently expect that of him in order to get help with the younger siblings. If he is the youngest, he must compete with his siblings and constantly prove his maturity, so he may insist on doing things he is too young to do. If he is the middle child, he may act out to get attention that his younger and older siblings seem to hog, at least in his mind.

Your child knows when something is unfair. He will become resentful as a result. Explain to him your logic to prove to him that something is not unfair.

A strong-willed child likes to be independent and feels insulted when you remind him of things. Give him a list of things to accomplish to make him feel independent. Let him pick his own outfits and make his own meal selection when you go out to eat.

Your child relies on you to make him feel important and heard. Listen to him and praise him to help him grow his self-esteem.

Your child wants your respect and will fight with you to earn it. Treating him with respect involves speaking to him like an adult, asking for his input like a valued member of the family, giving him his independence, and not cussing at him or speaking to him rudely.

He needs a solid routine to guide his behavior. With a routine, he knows what you expect of him. This eliminates some of the tantrums he may throw out of confusion or stress.

Give him choices and honor them. For instance, ask what he wants to do before bedtime: Watch a movie, read a book, or sing songs?

Let him learn from experience. This is the best, and often only, way that strong-willed children learn. You may want to shield him from pain or unpleasantness, but he will become rebellious if you coddle him.

When he gets upset, show him how to regulate his emotions in a healthy way. No, screaming and cussing is not a good way to express rage. Talking about things or taking frustration out by focusing energy on a project is far better.

Think of how everyone can benefit. This can be tough when you have more than one child to consider, but be creative and flexible. Explain to your strong-willed child that he is not the only one in the household and he must be mindful of others and reach a solution that makes everyone happy.

Your life will change when you have children, period. A strong-willed wild child will particularly upset the status quo and challenge you as a person and a parent. The best parents are not perfect. They just accept the situation they have to deal with and learn from their mistakes. You can explain that to your child honestly and ask him for patience as you learn to parent him in the best way. Teach him that mistakes are normal and that you can bounce back from anything.

Chapter 7: How To Foster Identity

When dealing with strong-willed children, one of the issues parents struggle to overcome is their children's strive for identity.

Strong-willed children have a tendency to fight for their identity just that bit harder.

One of the great pieces of advice I can give any parent is this **"your child is not you"**.

Yes, we are parents, and we have a responsibility to help shape choices, but that doesn't mean we should make all the main decisions for them.

Allowing children to make their own decisions is crucial in them shaping their future character and identity.

I have talked to many parents who treat their children as if they are miniature versions of themselves, whose sole purpose in the universe is to re-live their failed lives and fantasies. I have seen parents whose worldview has clouded their objectivity.

The old adage is **"the father's prayer is that his sons should be greater than he"**. We remember Albert Einstein, Bill Gates and Isaac Newton. But does anyone remember who their parents were?

The point is that very often children learn from their parents and often surpass their parents in many ways, and every loving parent should wish this should be the case.

The world is constantly changing, and the rules are constantly changing too, so we should guide our children and instill the values in them that will allow them to continue to be successful in the world they find themselves long after they fly the nest.

Regardless of how noble and lofty our ambitions are for our children; we must realize that our role is not to carve out their destiny but to help them create a life that will bring them fulfillment.

As parents, we really need to be careful not to kill our children's creativity and individuality especially if they are passionate about things we do not understand.

One thing is for sure a strong-willed child is very resolute about their individual passion and identity, and you must learn how to foster their development rather than destroying it.

Children may develop different dominant character traits. Some are introverts while some are extroverts. Some children are confident while others are shy and lacking in confidence. Some children are hard-working and some are lazy and unmotivated.

Regardless if they dominant character traits we must allow them to freedom of finding their own identities without being over-bearing.

If you are confident naturally and your child does not exhibit the same traits, do not make them feel something is wrong with them because they are shy. The best way to deal with traits we do not like is to create an environment for development that does not make the child feel judged or below our expectations. Our job is to create a forum in which they can express themselves at least to their nuclear family.

A self-confident child will feel free to express their feelings about something. However, when the child has a low self-esteem, they often become withdrawn and do not open up about what is bothering them. Parents can foster expression and individuality in children by being supportive. But first, they have to understand their children for who they are. Parents need to recognize the uniqueness of their children and not try to force them to what they are not. Both internal and external forces can affect a child's personality. It is the duty of the parent to offer guidance to the child so that the child can be able to make his/her own choices without feeling pressured.

How to foster individuality in a child?

When children are still young, they try to mimic your behavior in the process of learning what the appropriate behavior is. The child's world slowly grows and soon they start mimicking other children's behavior. When they join the school, they realize that they are part of a larger group. They try to figure out how they can "fit in." You can guide your children into being unique in their own way.

Here are some strategies that parents can use when they want their children to have better behavior in the process of finding themselves.

Understand your child's perspective

When your child imitates another child's behavior, it isn't a bad thing. In so doing, they adjust their own behavior. You can try to figure out why they mimic that person. There has to be something that makes them desire to be like them. Maybe there are some other children that your child doesn't like, and so he would try to adjust his behavior so as to differentiate himself from them. Other children just want to get the same reaction that the other child gets. It could be the words that they use that make people laugh.

Prevent peer pressure

Children who are not comfortable doing their own things can easily become vulnerable to peer pressure. That is why it is important for a parent to urge their child to be comfortable doing their own thing. Since many people spend a lot of time in groups in school, they try to conform so that they can dress, speak or act like the other members of the group. These groups can be very influential in changing a person's lifestyle. Some groups can influence hairstyle, hair color, piercings in different parts of the body, tattoos, sexual relations, etc. They find comfort in such groups and would like to maintain their relationship; no matter what. If you let your child know that being different is okay, they will not be under pressure to do other things that they feel uncomfortable doing, just to please their friends. When your child draws, dances, sings or does any other activity, let them know that it is okay even if they do it differently from how others do it. However, this doesn't mean that you should teach your child does not have friends. Let your child know that despite the differences, they can still find common ground with friends.

Share your opinions with your child

Connect and communicate with your child and let them know what you feel about certain things that concerning his/her behavior. For instance, if your child has picked up a bad behavior from his/her friends, emphasize on the importance of good behavior. If your child starts using an inappropriate word that he/she heard from the friend, explain to your child why this word is bad and why he/she shouldn't use it anymore. Your child will have reason to believe that you are right. When your child imitates, she is just experimenting. It doesn't mean that they will always be followers. As long as you show them some guidance, they will more likely choose good role models to emulate.

Make an Impression

When your child isn't in school, you can monitor whom he/she spends time with that influences their behavior. It doesn't have to be someone. It could be something. If there are any children that you feel that can be a good example to your child, schedule a play date with your child. You want them to interact so that they can learn from each other about a thing or two. You should also engage in family activities, which foster good core values. It could be about giving back to the society, volunteering, etc. your child can learn how to treat others by observing and listening to how you treat other people.

You should therefore, be a good role model so that your child can emulate these positive things.

How you can encourage your child's individuality

Let them have a say in what they wear. Let them develop their own style by allowing them to pick what they can put on. If the child is too young, you can select two pieces of clothes and ask your child to choose one.

You should not dwell so much on what your neighbors are saying. This may prompt you to change the character of your child forcefully.

Encourage your child to explore their identity.

Even if he/she takes some strange direction, it is still okay. At least, they are thinking about something unique for themselves.

Accept your children for who they are. What is meant to be will be. You should not have a setup agenda for your child's future. For instance, when your child is young, don't fixate your mind into believing that your child will be a doctor. Don't force your child into taking a direction that they are not interested in. Let them be guided by their interests. As they grow, you can give them some pieces of advice, but you shouldn't force them to be what they are not or do not want. Celebrate their achievements in whichever field.

Take note of your child's likes, interests, talents, preferences, and attributes. It can help you in guiding them to do that which their heart desires. Encourage your child to go after their dreams. Let them know that they can make it. Listen to your child so that you can know about their aspirations.

Accept that the two of you are a different and you may have different likes or dislikes. Do not force your child to like what you like. Your child may dislike the things that you like. Know that your child is a unique being and not an extension of you.

Do not make comparisons between your child and others.

Do not compare him/her to yourself. Siblings can be very different. Do not compare them. This will create sibling rivalry, which can get nasty at times. It also breeds jealousy and hatred between siblings. Your child may begin to feel that he/she is not good enough especially if you keep saying how the other sibling is far much better in many ways.

Examine how you are attached to their interests, appearance, and goals. How do you want your child to look or to present herself/himself to the public? Are you okay with it? Are you embarrassed by their choices?

Encourage your child to explore new things.

When they are excited about an activity that they are part of, like the drama club, school choir, cheerleading, etc., share in their excitement and be supportive. Attend their performances and encourage them to keep going.

How to build self-esteem by fostering individuality?

When a parent allows his/her child to express their individuality the healthy way, the child's self-esteem will improve. The major conflict that most children face is figuring out if they should do what other people want them to, or if they should do that which they want for themselves. Some external forces can influence the child's character. These include demands from parents as well as peer pressure and media marketing. Children have to be guided in knowing the difference between needs and wants. Parents can help their children know that what is important in a person is their character and not their possessions. Once children identify things that are important to them, they will develop their own character. This will strengthen their sense of individuality.

Encourage extracurricular activities

Sometimes life isn't just about books and books alone. Find out which activity your child enjoys most. This will help them discover their strengths.

Do not be critical

We all make mistakes. When your child makes a mistake, address the issue in a reasonable way. Do not make your child feel bad about himself/herself. Let your child know that mistakes do not mean failure, but they are learning experiences. If your child says negative comments concerning them, help by re-framing them. Turn them into positive statements.

Praise efforts

Let your child know that the focus in on the process and not the end result. It doesn't matter how the end result would be, what matters is the process. Praise your child for participating in various activities.

Encourage exercises

Many people, including children, can be affected by their body image. For instance, if they are overweight, they will not be comfortable to interact with others in public spaces. They will feel that people are constantly talking about them. This will make them isolated and would not want to talk about their feelings. They will become dormant. Some get picked at while at school. All these have a negative impact on their self-esteem. That is why a parent has to ensure that the children live healthy lives by encouraging them to do regular exercises.

Encourage your children to join clubs, organizations, and teams. This will give them a sense of belonging. Examples include youth groups, girl guides, sporting clubs, theatre groups, etc.

Chapter 8: Getting Along With Your Teens

So when they were little, your kids would follow you everywhere and you couldn't even go to the restroom in peace. But suddenly they hit their teens and they want to be left alone. What happened? Did you do something wrong?

Welcome to puberty, raging hormones and everything else that comes with the teenage years. You probably felt the same way when you were a teen. They also have emotional outbursts like when they were younger, but this time it is made more complicated by their drastically changing environment, and the fact that much of what they do and what they think of is no longer under your control.

No matter how difficult it can get during tough times, having teens is also rewarding because their increased understanding of the world also allows for more mature communication between the two of you. They are capable of taking responsibilities, can aid you in household matters and taking care of their younger siblings. Developing friendships with your teenagers may be very hard at first, but can be one of the most enjoyable moments of your parenthood. Here are some tips to make things work:

When they say they need space, they really do – This is the peak of discovering who they really are and defining who they want to be. As much as you would like to be there every step of the way, you're better off not doing so because they need to feel in charge. You need to step back and trust that they can do it.

Know their friends – A sad fact is their friends influence them as much as you do, maybe even more than you do. Know who they are with but never judge their friends because you alienate yourself from your teenager when you do so. When you find that one of their friends is a dangerous influence, try talking about this to your teen, but make sure to criticize the behavior and not the person. Besides, being close to your teenager's friends makes your own child closer to you, and they feel more responsible for their actions because of the trust you give them.

Set limits and define consequences – This teaches the child to be more responsible and aware with what they do. Define the rules, and what happens when they break it. Make sure to stick with these rules to let them know that you mean business and that you really mean everything you say.

Allow them to reason out – At one point your children will learn to answer back and you will have long arguments, but this is necessary to make them understand how you make your decisions. This is also a way to show them that you acknowledge what they think about key situations. However, be firm and don't be afraid to reprimand when they start answering with disrespect because at the end of the day you're still their parents.

Presence, presence, presence – it doesn't matter if you just sit next to each other without making groundbreaking discussions. Doing things together, even the most mundane of activities, gives them the security that you're always there. And when they say they need to talk – make an effort to really allot time for it because at this phase, you won't get to do this very often.

Sibling Rivalry – while this may be child's play when they were young, sibling rivalry can get more complicated in their teens as their feelings of insecurity are magnified and some of their angst may be directed to their own brothers and sisters. This is a complicated matter altogether but the key to this is the time you spend with each kid, and the effort that both parents put in getting to know their interests and the way the perceive things. This shouldn't depend on who gets the most medals or who gives their parents the least headaches. Every child is entitled to that same attention.

That being said set a forum among your children so they could discuss their conflicts with each other. This is a great exercise to prepare them for the outside world. Mediate, but try your best to not directly interfere when they fight, as it may only make matters worse.

Chapter 9: How Do I Deal With My Teenager's Fluctuating Moods?

Many times, moodiness is just a part of growing up. Your teenager may be going through hormonal changes that they don't even understand, and it makes them a lot grumpier than they mean to be. Dealing with moods may be difficult for you, because a lot of times they direct their moodiness toward you, the parent. Your reaction may be to get upset and angry back, but that's not going to fix anything. That's why you need to understand how to better deal with your teenager's fluctuating moods.

If your teenager seems to be getting moody at the oddest times, make sure that you take the time to talk to them. See if there's something that you can do in order to help them deal with their emotions. Obviously, if they're just getting irritated by little things that you or your spouse are doing, you can't really help that, but if there's something big going on, you can play a role in helping them ease that stress a bit.

Another way to deal with moodiness is to let your teenager talk it out. The teenage years are a time where they are just learning how to deal with their emotions in a healthy manner. So helping them learn how to interpret their feelings is just as important as teaching them how to express them in a way that doesn't hurt other people. So don't get mad right back at them; sit them down, let them express their feelings and let them know that you care about them and are able to help them work through all of these wild and crazy changes.

Usually, the fluctuating moods are a sign of a healthy transition into adulthood. There are rare cases, however, where you need to remember that not all moodiness is a result of hormones. There are cases where the moodiness is the sign of a deeper problem. This, of course, is something that parents don't want to think about. But, many teenagers go through bouts of depression and anxiety during their teenage years. Unfortunately, this has become a regular part of the teenage experience for many people. The teenage years are when, if your child is suffering from mental illness, it starts to rear its ugly head.

So what do you do if you are concerned that there are bigger problems going on? What do you do if you're concerned that there may be some issues with mental illness? Then it may be time for you to consider taking your child to see a counselor, psychologist, or psychiatrist. The good thing is, if there is a problem going on and you find it early, your teenager will be able to get the treatment that they need in order to thrive in today's world. If you try to ignore it, it will just cause more problems for your teenager while they are transitioning into adulthood.

Like any sort of illness, catching it early helps to prevent further complications. Remember, even if they are struggling with depression or anxiety now, they may not deal with it for the rest of their lives, especially if they get the help that they need early on. So look around your community and get suggestions on which therapists that you should consider for your child. Let them be part of the process; if they are getting frustrated with the way they feel, they're going to be a lot more receptive to getting the help that they need. Remember, you can't help someone that doesn't want to be helped, but as a parent, you can take your child to see a professional without having to get signatures and such. They may be resentful for a time, but they will work past it when they realize how helpful and beneficial the therapy will be for their overall wellbeing.

Chapter 10: Your Child's Training And Discipline

Best Discipline Techniques

Establish an emotional connection early. It is important for parents to understand that a healthy relati0nship between parent and child is the very foundation of discipline. In order to know how to discipline your toddler, you first need to understand him. This is often referred to as attachment parenting. By becoming an expert on your own child, you have a better idea on what appropriate approach to use and how to best convey your expectations.

Get to know your child. No two children are alike, so take time to study your child. It is important to fully understand his particular needs and capabilities are every stage of his development. As the child grows, you will need to use different discipline techniques. The tantrum of a two year old requires a different approach than that of an eight year old.

A lot of conflicts arise when parents expect their children to behave like adults. You need to define and learn to differentiate an appropriate behavior of a specific age from misbehavior. As a parent, it is important to learn to tolerate behaviors that go along with the child's age and development stage (for example, one cannot expect a two year old toddler to sit still for a long time), but correct insolence and disrespectful behavior.

Help your child to recognize and respect authority. Parents take full charge of their children, that's the basic in discipline. However, being a trusted and respected authority does not automatically come with your job as a parent. Telling your child to obey "or else" may temporarily work, but it is accomplished out of fear and not out of respect.

So how does one gain this respect? As an authority figure, a parent needs to be warm and yet wise. Connect with your child as a nurturer and a comforter. In doing so, you will win the trust of your toddler. Do not confuse being in charge as being in control. Instead of imposing full control over your toddler, focus on controlling the situation to make it easier for your child to control himself.

Provide structure by setting limits. Early on, establish some ground rules, and do not forget to create conditions that will make your rules easier for your child to follow. Children, as they grow and explore the world on their own need clearly defined boundaries. For example, constantly saying "no" to a highly inquisitive toddler who loves to explore will only fall to deaf ears. Provide structure and set limits by childproofing your home in order to nurture curious minds and provide him a safe place to learn and play.

Expect obedience. Keep in mind that a toddler is as obedient as you can possibly expect or can be as defiant as you can possibly allow. Children become more obedient by knowing their parents expect them to.

Handling Toddler Freakouts

It is astonishing how one small kid can easily create a big scene in public. Truth is, even if your child has a generally sweet disposition and a mild temperament, meltdowns and freakouts are inevitable; it is a fact of toddler life that parents need to learn how to deal with. For parents, it is important to understand that tantrums do not reflect your parenting skills. Your child simply wants to show his frustration. Here are some effective ways to handle tantrums without losing your cool:

What Triggers Tantrums

In most cases, you may think your toddler is having a meltdown for no obvious reasons. But the truth is, there are real causes for these tantrums. Keep in mind that toddlers have difficulty expressing what they feel and what they want. An eight year old can freely express preference on the choice of food or the color of cup he wants to use for his apple juice, but toddlers may scream bloody murder just to get his point across.

Toddlers are also easily overwhelmed. They thrive on routines, which means a slight deviation will easily throw them off. For instance, missing a naptime by 10 minutes can be a recipe for disaster. Toddlers are also naturally curious beings and most of the time, their bodies cannot keep pace with their innate curiosity. You can just imagine their frustration when told they are not allowed to climb the kitchen stool.

Toddlers also do not understand delayed gratification. Kids this age live in the moment, which means promising cookies after dinner will not work. Not getting what they want and when they want it is a primary trigger for a tantrum.

How to Diffuse Tantrums

1. **First, you need to acknowledge your child's frustration.** Look your child in the eye and recognize his pain and frustration. You can start by saying, "I know you want to eat that cookie", or "I know you are upset", then assure him that you will help make him feel better. It is important to keep calm and composed. You can then add, "I wish we can have cookies, too. But it's too bad we can't have one right now."

2. **Be silly.** Laughter is one important weapon to effectively diffuse tantrums. If you feel your toddler is working up a temper, do something silly that will make him laugh or giggle.

3. **Try distraction.** Diverting his attention will force him to focus on something else. For example, if you are having trouble convincing your tot to leave the park, be creative in presenting a diversion such as "How many dogs do you think we will pass by on our way home?"

4. Ignore. Sometimes, tantrums will easily escalate when your child thinks he can get what he wants if he will scream loud enough. If you will not react, then he may eventually give up.

5. Leave the scene. When all tantrum-diffusing strategies fail to work, leave the scene without making a major fuss. It is important that you still exude calm. This will teach your child that you are still in control.

Top Tantrum Stoppers

A day in a park can easily turn out to be a nightmare if you have a toddler in tow. With other kids around, your toddler can break down into a fit if other kids won't let him borrow a toy. Making an attempt to reason with your child under disapproving eyes of other parents can be quite unnerving, to say the least. Here are some practical tips on how to prevent your toddler from making a scene:

1. Start off smart. Recognize and diffuse a tantrum before they even start. Role-playing with your child at home will teach him how to respond to various situations. It is important for him to understand that not all kids will willingly share their toys.

2. Establish expectations. Most times, kids throw tantrums when they do not get their way. Before leaving the house, inform your toddler that you are both going out to buy some food, but you will not buy him a new toy. You can ask your child to repeat this piece of information back to you and keep discussing this with him on your way to the supermarket.

3. Be prepared. When going out, always pack some light snack for your toddler to munch on. You can't expect to drag your child along with you shopping and expect him to stay serene and cheerful. When in restaurants, it may take too long to serve appetizers, so be sure to have a stash of nibbles to keep him happy.

4. Don't give in. Tantrums usually happen when parents easily give in too often and too soon. You don't want to teach your child that they can use tantrums to get what they want.

5. Be consistent. If you are able to handle tantrums at home successfully, public tantrums will gradually lessen.

Correcting Toddler Behavior

It can be quite shocking, but toddlers can resort to aggressive behaviors such as hitting, throwing and biting. This is in fact a normal part of your child's development, particularly in learning self-control. Typically, toddlers will eventually grow out of such behaviors when they reach age four. However, it doesn't mean you can just ignore and endure it. It is important for your child to know and understand that aggressive behaviors are unacceptable. Here are some ways to correct them effectively:

Hitting

Toddlers share a common fascination of being able to make things happen and are constantly curious how people around them will react. Hitting people easily satisfies these two interests. Keep in mind that at this age, toddlers do not fully understand that other people also have different ideas and have feelings like they do. To deal with this:

• Don't be afraid to show your child you are angry. However, make sure to express your anger constructively, as a chance to teach a lesson and not to frighten him.

• Immediately stop aggression. Do not allow your child to hit you or someone else repeatedly. Firmly grip the wrist and say, "No hitting. You can be angry, but you are not allowed to hit me."

• Expect compliance. Don't let go of your child's wrist until you feel the tension leave his body. If he attempts to strike again, repeat steps above and hold his wrist longer and wait for him to fully relax.

- When he starts to relax, praise him. Give as well as ask for a hug. This does not mean you are letting them get away with it, but making them understand that it's okay to be angry, but they can express it in other ways.

Biting

Biting, while considered a normal phase, is not an acceptable behavior. Your toddler needs to understand this. Adults need to respond quickly by firmly stopping and correcting the behavior with a firm "no". It is also important to prevent biting before it occurs rather than dealing with it after it has happened.

Throwing

Toddlers are fascinated with cause and effect. Throwing spoons and cups is their way of testing gravity. It is important for parents to know that throwing does not necessarily mean your kid is acting out, nor is it an act of defiance or aggression.

Sometimes, it is a means of communication. For example, throwing a sippy cup may mean he wants more. Be more attuned to his needs.

Basic Guide to Potty Training

All parents look forward to saying goodbye to stinky diapers and most kids are excited to wear real underwear. Typically, toddlers show signs of potty training readiness between 18 and 24 months. Of course, this is not an overnight process. Here are some basic guidelines of potty training your child:

Is Your Child Ready to be Potty Trained?

You can start potty training when:

- Your child has learn words for stool, urine and toilet
- When he starts to show discomfort of feeling soiled or wet
- Shows interest and curiosity of using the potty
- Shows awareness when he is about to poo or pee

Are You Ready to Potty Train Your Child?

Potty training, unknown to many parents will require patience and energy. This means countless bathroom visits as well as extra laundry as well as puddle cleaning—all of which you are expected to take on with an encouraging smile.

If you or your spouse is not up to the challenge for some reason, do not feel bad postponing it. It is more important to wait until the timing is right.

Potty Training Strategies

1. Buy a potty

2. Introduce potty to your toddler

3. Have your kid sit on the potty clothed and unclothed

4. Buy a fun and colorful underwear

5. Learn to tailor your potty training strategy according to your child's temperament

The Hugs and Kisses Approach—praise your child for every successful trip to the potty by clapping your hands, giving hugs and kisses. You can also tell other family members so they can also fuss over him and give him due recognition.

The Cold Turkey Approach—ask your child to pick out some fun underpants. On the appointed day, make a grand production of putting it on him. This may mean doing several cleanups, especially on the first few days.

Teaching Your Child Some Manners

Teaching your child proper manners is a long and gradual process. It will require constant reminders before your child can fully learn and understand. However, one of the best ways to effectively inculcate good behavior is to be a good example. It will take a lot of patience before your toddler will eventually learn. Here are some helpful tips:

• To promote polite behavior, be consistently polite by never failing to say "please" and "thank you" at every opportunity.

- Effectively promote empathy by talking and making him understand how other people feel when they are hurt. You can exercise this every time you read bedtime stories. For example, explain how Cinderella is hurt because her two stepsisters were very mean to her.

- Gradually introduce the concept of turn taking and sharing.

- Make him use a bib when eating and train him to properly use spoon and fork.

- Remind your child to wash his hands before eating.

- Emphasize magic words such as "excuse me" and "you're welcome".

- Take time to rephrase things properly. For instance, your child says "I want a glass of water", you can correct this by saying, "May I have a glass of water, please?" and ask your toddler to repeat this.

- If you feel he is old enough, you can ask your toddler to help out on simple household chores such as bringing utensils to the table. This will introduce him to the concept of being helpful.

• Teach the art of sharing. Every time your child grabs a toy from another kid, gently remind him that it is not okay to grab a friend's toy without asking for permission. Ask him how would his friend feel every time he does this.

• Teach him when to use indoor and outdoor voice. This will make him understand when it is okay to be loud and when he needs to be quiet.

Teaching Your Child the Meaning of "No"

When it comes to teaching your toddler anything, it is very important for parents to take time to understand their kid's language as well as find out what makes them tick. The same applies when it comes to teaching your toddler the meaning of "no", which is a very important command that they need to understand and respect at an early age.

According to child experts, toddlers are known to respond best to verbal commands when they are followed by actions to emphasize its meaning. This is because, when it comes to dealing with toddlers, actions do speak louder than words. By making a physical follow through, you will be able to communicate the command better.

What Types of Follow-Through?

Experts highly recommend physical follow-through followed and enforced with behavioral follow-through. For instance, your toddler starts to climb over a table. Firmly say "no" then back this up with a physical action, which is removing him from the table. You can repeat saying "no" again and redirect your child's attention to something else. It is also important to praise him when he starts to engage in the '"right" activity. Using a physical and behavioral follow through will let your child understand you mean what you say every single time you say "no".

Save Your "No's" For Addressing Serious Issues

Fact is, if you frequently say "no", the word will eventually lose its meaning and power as a command. It is important for parents to reserve "no's" for some major situations in order to prevent devaluing the said word as well as keeping the meaning clear.

Explain the Word "No"

When saying "no", do not simply give out a simple exclamation. Instead, communicate exactly what you won't allow or forbid him to do. For example, you can say, "No, do not climb up the table". Never yell or spank you child while delivering the command "no", this will only make the child fear as well as create confusion, making those feelings cloud the real issue.

Chapter 11: General Health

The health of our children is one of the biggest sources of worry in a parent's life. When they were babies the smallest cough or cold was enough to have us rushing to the doctor. When they were toddlers there were cuts and bruises to be dealt with. Then as teenager's kids are always pushing the limits with sports, new experiences like drinking, and stresses associated with studying and work that bring a whole raft of new health challenges to our lives as parents. Keeping our kids healthy can be a challenge.

But once your teen leaves home, the responsibility for staying healthy is shifted to them. Of course you will still be there if they need you, but they will need to practice some healthy habits to stay healthy in the first place. So let's address some healthy habits that you can impart to your teen before they leave home.

Lesson #9: Exercise and Diet

Exercise is crucial in leading a healthy and sustainable lifestyle. It is relatively easy to stay fit as a teenager as school and university commitments are only for a few hours per day which leave ample time for sport and other forms of exercise. Metabolism rates in teenaged bodies are also relatively high to promote growth. This means that their bodies are able to process large amounts of food without it being turned into fat. Once you reach the end of your teenage years, as most of us have experienced, this all changes. Your metabolism slows down, your work takes up more of your time, and as a result you don't exercise as much and start to put on weight.

Before leaving home your teen should be aware of this and equipped with proper exercising and diet habits. They should be aware of the many health benefits of exercising, as well as the dangers of not exercising.

Lessons we want to teach about the value of Diet and Exercise

Diet

Your brain does not function without food and water to process for energy. You need to eat breakfast and rehydrate your body after sleeping in the morning to promote brain function.

Example: Going to an exam without breakfast. You might have done the study, but if you are hungry sometimes your brain just cannot make the connections between the questions you read and the answers that you have stored away. You need to eat to function.

You cannot consume as much as you did when you were a teenaged athlete when you hit your 20's and are working a full time job. There is lots of information that you can find online about this but one rule of thumb that I have is that males in their 20's require roughly 2,600 calories per day, and females requires 2,000.

http://healthyeating.sfgate.com/diet-20yearolds-2446.html

Exercise

Set a realistic goal. If they want to maintain their figure, want to become stronger, more toned, or pursue a specific sporting interest they first need to write it down as a goal.

Be consistent when exercising. Regardless of your goals, be it weight loss, or just keeping fit, you must never give up if you want proper results.

Instill in them the need to create and abide by a proper workout routine. The plan must also be compatible with their lifestyle; otherwise, it is not going to work.

It is also a good idea for them to get someone else who shares their goals to join them when exercising. This makes it fun and easier. You can be doing this with them just to make it a habit.

My children were completely different in their exercise and diet routines. My son was already heavily involved in sport and so I did not have to worry about him, but my daughter was much more academic focused and enjoys food so these lessons were vital to her.

By sitting down with her and discussing the benefits of exercise and relating my own experiences when I started work it avoided feeling like an attack on her personally. We agreed that she would take up running 2-3 times per week, and that if she kept it up for a month we would go out for a celebratory dinner.

Key Takeaways

Promoting a healthy diet and exercise routine in your child's life can prevent numerous health complications that come with being unfit. By regularly exercising your teen is much less likely to develop obesity, depression, certain kinds of cancer, and arthritis. As a parent I have been much happier letting my children leave home with the knowledge that they maintain healthy diet and exercise routines in their lives.

Every child will be different, and when you are addressing diet and exercise with your own it is important to try not to offend. Teenagers are quick to feel attacked and take offense to such advice. But if you can suggest a change in a nice way and sweeten any proposition with a reward to work towards then you are on track to successfully teaching your child what they need to hear.

Lesson #10: Sexual responsibility

One of the things that your kids leave your house for is sexual freedom. As a parent you may find it a struggle to accept that your child may be sexually active. I personally would avoid thinking of this as much as possible. But before your child leaves home it is your duty as a parent to bestow a sense of sexual responsibility and voice the consequences and dangers of sexual conduct to your teen.

Steps to take in teaching your children sexual responsibility

Define a healthy and an unhealthy relationship. It is important for them to know the value of sex, and the meaning of it.

Let them know about the laws and regulation associated with sex, and legal repercussions of failing to abide by those rules.

As paradox as it may sound, it is important to enforce the issue of safe sex. Condoms, birth control, and the need for discussing this with a potential partner.

Let them know the consequences of having unprotected sex such as sexually transmitted diseases, and unplanned pregnancies.

Once again these lessons are awkward and may already have been covered by the time your child is leaving home but they are necessary. I would really hope that in most cases they have already been covered. However you should take the time to enforce them. Make it clear that your expectation is for your child to be taking precautionary measures and that you do not want grandchildren before they are ready for them. But also make it clear that if they do have a problem that they can always come to you and ask for advice or for help.

Key Takeaways

You cannot assume that your child will be taught what is right and what is wrong by outside influences. You need to take personal responsibility for enforcing a message of sexual responsibility and the consequences that can arise from being careless when it comes to sex before your child leaves home. Being sexually responsible can help your child avoid embarrassing or overbearing situations in future such as unplanned pregnancies or STIs, which may have a significant impact on their lives.

Lesson #11: The importance of Medical Care

Being healthy is not a privilege. It is important that your kids know the value of medical care and the consequences of ignoring to see a doctor when they are in need of one.

Important lessons in medical care:

If your child is moving a significant distance away from your existing family doctor then encourage them to seek out and establish a relationship with a new GP. Once this is formally done your child's medical files will be transferred and be readily available should they be needed.

Locate and establish the contact details of the closest hospital in case of an emergency.

Recognition that symptoms such as sudden dizziness, being short of breath, confusion, chest pain, severe or persistent vomiting all warrant visiting a doctor or hospital straight away.

Do not accept any pills or prescription medication from friends or strangers to treat any symptoms that might be occurring. Incorrect dosage, allergies, and other problems can come of this so it is always best to consult a medical professional when in need of advice

If your child is moving to America or another country that requires health care insurance make sure that your child insures them self. Sit down and do the research and budgeting with them if necessary.

Key Takeaways:

Getting medical attention before a situation gets out of hand can prove to vital in so many scenarios. By making sure that your teen knows when to seek medical advice and how to do so they can potentially avoid letting a bad situation get worse. Knowing that your child has access to such resources and knowledge of when and how to use them will give you one less thing to worry about once they have moved out of home.

Lesson #12: Alcohol/Drug abuse

Alcohol and drugs are always a danger in society. As a parent I would love to tell you that your child will avoid problems with either, but I can't. Sometimes even the brightest, most straight laced children go down the wrong path. But what I can tell you is that giving your teen the information that they need to make an informed decision can help. It can give them the ammunition that they need to say no to peer pressure, to choose better friends, and to stay clear of abusing drugs and alcohol in their lives. The best time to tackle this problem is early on, while they are still living at home.

Steps to take:

Research about the various drugs out there so that you can get enough information to talk to your kids; you don't want to be look clueless on such important issues. You can do this by looking online for posts by professionals to get adequate and firsthand information on drug types and their side effects.

Teach them on the dangers of drug abuse and alcohol, but DO NOT tell them never to use drugs. Instead outline your expectation with regard to drinking and using drugs. E.g. If they have been drinking while at home and coming home drunk and out of control, then tell them exactly how you feel about that.

Be candid with your children. Let them know about any experiences with alcoholism or drug addiction that you have encountered and really highlight the negatives.

I personally have a family member who lost everything to a drug addiction some years ago. He was a relatively successful man who owned his own home and had a fairly well-paying job. After undergoing an operation he was prescribed morphine for the pain he experienced while healing. When the prescription ran out he craved more and eventually found himself trying Heroin.

From there his life spiraled out of control. He was fired from his job for trying to steal equipment to sell for drugs. He lost a significant amount of weight. A lot of his friends ceased contact with him. If it was not for some close family members that checked him into rehab against his will he most likely would have lost his house and been dead shortly after.

Key Takeaways

It is a horrible thing to witness someone going through a battle with alcoholism or drug addiction. It can quickly escalate from a good time to a life destroying event. For this reason it is vitally important to make your teen aware of the dangers of both drugs and alcohol before they move out of home. Once they gain their independence it is much easier to be influenced by peer pressure to try new things. Knowing the consequences of trying drugs like heroin and methamphetamines becomes the biggest deterrent that we as parents can pass on to our children.

Chapter 12: Behavioural Problems

The Root of the Problem

If your teenager suddenly appears to have lost their way and begins to exhibit behavior that is abnormal for them, then you will need to be able to skillfully ramp up your observations. In order to do so you will need to know basics of things like, symptoms of teenage depression.

Symptoms of teen depression are not limited to just the following, but some standard behaviors include: excessive sadness or moodiness, unexplained weight changes, loss of interest in school or social activities, excessive absences from school, unexplained physical aches and pains, sudden episodes of rage or guilt, decreased ability to concentrate, and even the choice, or preoccupation with dark color schemes for clothing, artwork and even decorations for their bedroom.

Assuming you're already on top of knowing who your child's friends are and where they spend their free time, this discussion will focus on behavior changes that are associated with a limited set of problems your teenager may be experiencing.

Most children are diagnosed with Attention Deficit Disorder, and other learning disabilities early on in the educational process. That is not to say that your child may not have such diagnoses, but the focus of this booklet will be to make parents more aware of the more affective disorders teens are susceptible to.

Affective disorders are commonly known as "mood disorders". They are things such as depression and anxiety. The discussion of bipolar disorder (that is also an affective disorder) is beyond the scope of this booklet.

Nonetheless, if a teen is experiencing major mood swings it is highly recommended, that parents seek medical attention for their teenager in order to rule out such a serious disorder.

Teen depression exhibits itself in several different ways depending on the person and the severity of the episode.

Parents may not realize the impact that stress can have on their growing teenager. We often hear the term, "Drama Queen". To the most "normal" teenager having things go wrong in their life can be extremely stressful.

If a stressful event is coupled with the feeling that there is little to nothing the teen can do to change the situation, then the result may be fertile ground for the their feeling helpless.

The more the teen dwells on the situation, without adult counsel and intervention the more likely they are to fall into an unhealthy mood that may lead toward depression.

It doesn't always take an earth-shaking event to put a teenager into a mild depression. However, parents need to be especially mindful of drastic life changes and events that affect or threaten their teenagers' feelings of security.

Such events may include, but not be limited to events like long distance moves, marital problems between the parents, death of a friend or relative, or even the passing of a favorite pet.

Recognizing how fragile some teenager's psyche is, when there is a traumatic event in a school or community, that directly affects students, modern school districts readily provide professional counseling as a precautionary measure.

Additionally, long term monitoring of academic, social and energy levels of teenagers, who have experienced traumatic events in their lives, have proven to pay off in terms of mitigating further disruption to schools and communities.

Other considerations that may affect teenagers and impair their brain development is issues such as fetal alcohol syndrome, traumatic brain injury (even mild concussions from sports) and possible chemical imbalances from everything from undiagnosed medical conditions to recreational drug use.

The most important thing is that parents keep an open mind and be determined to intervene on their child's behalf – regardless of what the problem is.

If your teenager is diagnosed with depression, by a mental health professional, the treatment may include regular therapy sessions or even medication if the depression sets in for an extended period of time. In such an event parents can best help their depressed teen by first recognizing that the teenager is in need of treatment, and then by being persistent in following up with whatever treatment is prescribed for their child.

Usually depression will pass on its own, but be aware if your teenager is experiencing prolonged episodes of depression. We wont go into all the ramifications of prolonged depression, but I can tell you we had a close call with attempted suicide with our son so don't blow it off if you suspect depression in your teen.

If Not Depression - then WHAT?

Factors that cause behavioral problems can be as complex as diagnosed or undiagnosed behavior disorders, or as simple as normal, healthy teenage rebellion. Consequently, the "root" of teenaged behavioral problems can be wide and varied. Parents most often find their teens' behavioral problems manageable, but when their teenager is completely out of control it is imperative that professional help be brought in.

Regardless of the cause, if behavioral disorders are caught early enough parents can most likely help their child effectively deal with the symptoms. The cause of interruptive behavior is not always isolated, but mental health professionals can be of great assistance when the family cannot manage their teen's behaviors on their own.

If you're confident that your teen is not exhibiting symptoms of a behavioral disorder, but is just attention seeking then, by all means give him the attention he craves.

Additionally, try to redirect his energy into a healthy activity such as extracurricular activities at school, church youth groups, summer camps, a part time job, or possibly community service where he will be made to feel appreciated for his efforts.

We all like to feel acknowledged, and that is especially important for children. They will go to great lengths to get an adults attention, so the sooner you meet their need for your attention the better the outcome will be.

We've identified a few possible issues your teenager could be facing. However, the point I most want to stress to parents is that behaviors are simply symptoms of deeper issues.

It's often the method that a teen chooses to express their feelings of anger, rebellion, confusion, frustration or whatever that causes parents to flip their wig, start the loud lecturing and get side tracked.

In the bigger picture the wise parent focuses on the solution – not the problem. Therefore, the best defense a parent has against unacceptable behaviors is conversation. You must keep in mind that your ability to effectively communicate with your child is absolutely essential if you want to dig down deep into their heart and soul and find the "root" of their problem.

The worst of behaviors is, at the end of the day, nothing more than a symptom of a more serious problem. It's up to you, as the parent to discern whether or not you can resolve the problem on your own or whether you need to seek outside help.

When you are sincere about communicating with your child you will open your ears, and tape your mouth closed. Remember, your teen no more wants to hear what you have to say than you want to hear what they have to say. Each of you thinks you know the solution for a quick fix to the problem.

The REAL problem is – you don't know what the problem is until you first listen to your teenager. Your teen is likely poorly skilled at expressing his feelings and thoughts, so stay calm and be patient. You have to treat this session with your child as if you're an investigator trying to get all the facts.

It's unacceptable for an investigator to put words in a witness's mouth. They repeatedly use terms such as, "and then what happened?"

They use open-ended questions that do not require a yes or no answer. "So, what do you think would help?" or "So, what would you like me to do?" A good investigator's initial purpose is to gather as much information as they can. Only after that do they move on to trying to put the pieces of the puzzle together. I can't stress enough, that the questioning phase of an investigation is a total separate step to that of analyzing the information gathered.

Investigators repeat back what they think they are hearing with phrases like, "so, if I'm understanding you correctly... or just to be clear what your telling me is...." Another technique is to simply repeat ONE word of something they've said to get them to elaborate more on what they're trying to say.

This is your child, they will never stop being your child – as the saying goes, you've been given a lifetime sentence without time off for good behavior. In other words, you're in this for the long haul.

Try to be respectful, try to keep your focus on one issue or grievance at a time and most of all try to be objective and DON'T EXPLODE, regardless of what you hear. Believe me, I completely understand that you're likely dealing with a kid who has little appreciation for the blood, sweat and tears you've invested into his life, but your staying calm will pay higher dividends in the long run.

Take heart, these teen years will pass, so stay in there and don't give up. Keep in mind that sometimes teens will respond better to outsiders. You have to make the call of whether or not you need reinforcements, but experience tells me that communicating with the child (inside the almost adult body) is your greatest challenge. Once you master real communication – all the other problems will more quickly get resolved.

Chapter 13: Single Mom - Rewards For Good Behavior Kids Will Love

Positive behavior is what every parent aims to develop in their children during their tender years so that they will become fully functioning adults who are well-adjusted to their environment. Among toddlers, positive behavior is a consequence of the positive influences around them such as the good behavior of their parents. Likewise, the negative behavior of children is the result of negative influences they have been exposed to in their environment.

The parent's primary role in so far as child rearing is concerned is to filter out the negative influences and motivate their children to focus on the positive influences to develop positive behavior. Positive behavior is what will help the children transition from one development stage to another until they reach adulthood. By tradition, parents encourage their kids to develop positive behavior by rewarding them every time they did something good or positive. Likewise, to discourage them from being swayed by negative influences parents punish their kids for every negative behavior they manifest. The system of reward and punishment is the traditional way of encouraging the positive development of children which parents have used for ages because it has been proven to be effective.

And in so far as rewards for good behavior is concerned, parents are convinced that children, motivated by rewards, are likely to repeat a good deed over and over again until it becomes part of their nature. In a way, we can say then that reward is a consequence of good behavior and is definitely a major factor that motivates and influences children to acquire and develop good behavior.

Children love to be rewarded. They love candies too. They also enjoy food a lot.

And so for a long time, parents have used food and candies as rewards for good behavior. Unfortunately, as people became more conscious of their health, they started to realize that giving food as reward for good behavior also encourages unhealthy eating habits and a dissipated lifestyle.

Parents today are now in the lookout for positive reinforcements other than food to recognize the good behavior of their children and to encourage them to continue doing the good deed. And this is not without a good reason. In the first place, today's children are already drowning with unhealthy food choices. They are already at risk of being overweight in the future which may even lead to more serious health problems in the future.

Giving food or sweet treats like candy as reward encourages children to eat even if they are not hungry - an unhealthy eating habit that they may carry over into the various stages of their development. Instead of encouraging our children to make the healthy food choices we are actually encouraging them to adopt unhealthy eating habits.

As parents, single moms must not only be concerned with their kids' behavior but must be concerned with their health as well. Kids love to be rewarded. Rewards are effective in reinforcing good behavior. However, rewards as positive reinforcements must not be at the expense of the kids' health.

A single mom can actually come up with tons of ideas that can make his child happy and encourage good behavior at the same time. All he needs to do is tap into his creative mind. The only limit to what positive reinforcements he can come up with is his imagination.

The best way to start is to ask your child what he wants or what will make him happy. In other words, let your child make the list himself and you'll be surprised at how simple and inexpensive are the things that can make him happy.

Some of these ideas may be as simple as the following:

Your kid will love it if

You can read his favorite book to him.

You take him to the library.

You listen to him read.

You bring him to the park.

You spend quality time with him alone.

You play catch ball or catch Frisbee with him.

You give him a high five or a thumbs up.

You tell him he did a good job.

You give him a hug.

You give him permission to stay up late and watch TV.

You give him a special plate or placemat during dinner.

You give him a coloring book.

You add to his collection of rocks, stamps, etc.

You give him attractive stickers.

You let him pick the story or movie for family time.

You give him stuff he likes such as modeling clay, stuffed toys, large crayons, Mylar balloons, marbles, trading cards, etc.

You let him plan a family outing.

You will never run out of creative ideas you can use as alternative rewards for good behavior - but never forget to add some words of praise or appreciation like 'That was a great job, I am proud of you'. You'll be surprised at how much more motivated he will be to do more good deeds.

To make your reward system more fun and enjoyable, you can give it a twist by creating a "**I've been good**" jar. Get a big, transparent jar and fill it with things that will make him happy – like small toys, art supplies – things he has listed. Seeing the jar filled with goodies that will make him happy is encouraging enough and will motivate him to do a good deed so he can be rewarded with his choice of goodies from it. Keep adding new stuff into the jar so his interest won't wane.

Chapter 14: Discipline

Discipline is so vital to your child's success!!! BEATING, YELLING, and SCREAMING are not the only ways to discipline your child. These are also ways that should be used as least as possible. If you discipline appropriately from the beginning you will minimize your amount of extreme discipline. Remember just because you were disciplined a certain way does not mean it was the right way or the way you should discipline your child. The most crucial part of discipline is communicating to your child why what they did is wrong and proper behavior to exhibit. Kids can understand way more than you know; you just have to explain it to them.

Having different layers of discipline

Discipline does not have to be a one response action. It will make your life easier as a parent when you develop a system. Some ideas include decreasing time on electronics or taking away spending money when traveling. These systems will save you energy. The responsibility is yours to uphold the system consistently. Sometimes it can be hard because you want to see your kids smile and be happy all the time but a discipline system will enable them to achieve happiness throughout life. A system of discipline also increases the effectiveness of your highest punishment. If you fly off the handle every time your child does something wrong, you will severely weaken the effectiveness. You want your elite-level punishment to be rare but highly effective.

Being Consistent

As mentioned earlier you must be consistent in your discipline. Your kids will adjust to what you do. If you make threats or promises to them and do not follow through they will learn to manipulate you. Kids will continue to do whatever wrong thing that they did before, knowing that you will cave in on your discipline. Say specifically what you mean and mean exactly what you say then carry it out.

Stop Trying To Be Best Friends

Stop trying to be your child's best friend before being their parent. Unlike some people I think you can be your child's friend but ONLY if you are there parent first. Your primary job is to provide guidance to your child. That is showing real love to your child. Love is not just letting them do whatever they want, it is actually guiding them to do what they need.

More Freedom with Boundaries

One of the best analogies that I have seen that reveals this title is a reference to a fence.

"There was a school that was right by a decently trafficked street. Though there was grass on the front lawn the kids had to stay near the building when leaving the building for safety. The kids could not play on the grass because the cars and street were too close. Then one day a fence was built around the grass. Once, the fence was built the kids could enjoy all the grass on the front lawn because there was a fence to protect them from running into the street.

Your kids will feel safer and healthier when you institute boundaries. They may reject the idea at first but eventually when you hold firm it will help them. Freedom is not doing whatever you want; true freedom is having control over your actions and choices in life. Boundaries will also help guide your child and give them a better understanding of right and wrong.

Chapter 15: Discipline Strategies For Toddlers

So what does it mean to discipline a toddler? Some people believe this equates to giving a spanking and punishments, but that's not what discipline is. Discipline is about setting rules to keep your toddler from engaging in aggressive behavior, dangerous behavior, and inappropriate behavior. It's about making sure you follow through with the consequences when he or she breaks those rules. In this chapter, you're going to learn seven strategies that will help you set the limits and stop a toddler's bad behavior without resorting to punishments and spankings.

#1 Pick Battles

If you're always telling your toddler 'no,' then your toddler is going to tune out this word and not understand your priorities. In addition, you can't follow through with all of those 'no's.' Define what a priority to you is, set your limits, and follow through with the same consequences. Ease up on the little things that are kind of annoying, but fall into that 'who cares' category. For example, does your toddler like to wear a certain color all the time, or maybe they like to play a certain game all the time? Ease up on that and allow them to do it.

#2 Know Their Triggers

Some misbehavior from toddlers is completely preventable, as long as you anticipate what's going to spark their behavior. If you do, then you can make a game plan in advance, such as removing the temptations from them. This strategy works well if your toddler is fixated on misbehaving the same way every time. For example, if you know your toddler is going rip the candy off the shelves at the checkout line in the store, then put them in the cart where they can't reach the candy to make sure they can't get into trouble. Sometimes, avoidance is the better option.

If your toddler tends to grab cans off the grocery store shelves, then bring some toys along for them to play with in the cart as you shop. If your toddler doesn't share during playdates, then remove the specific toys he or she doesn't want to share from the play area. If your toddler likes to draw on the walls, then stash the crayons out of their reach when you're not supervising them during drawing time.

#3 Be Consistent

During the toddler stage, children are working hard to comprehend how their behavior impacts those around them. If your reaction to a situation changes all the time, you'll confuse your toddler with mixed signals. For example, if you allow your toddler to throw a ball in the house one day and change your mind the next, it's pretty confusing for their developing minds.

There isn't a timetable as to how many misbehaviors and consequences it will take before a toddler stops a certain behavior. However, if you respond the same way all the time, then they will learn the lesson after a few times. Consistency is the key for most toddlers.

A special warning for parents who have the cutesy toddler. All toddlers are cute, but if your toddler likes to use their cuteness to distract you, don't let them! This teaches them they can use this type of behavior to get away with anything, even as adults.

#4 Don't Become Emotional

It's difficult to stay calm when your toddler refuses to brush their teeth for the hundredth time in a row that week, or when they pull on the dog's tail after you told them not to six times that day. However, if you scream in anger, the message you send is lost in the escalating situation. When your toddler is flooded with your negative emotions, your toddler sees the emotions and doesn't understand what you're saying. They're too focused on the entertainment value of seeing you scream and yell as if you were the one throwing a fit, which you are. Therefore, resist that urge to raise your voice, count to three as you take a deep breath, and get down to their eye level. The reprimand for their behavior should be done in an even, but serious, tone.

#5 Keep It Short and Simple

For most first-time parents, they tend to reason with their toddler when they break the rules, offering a detailed explanation of what happened and issuing detailed threats about the privileges that will be lost if the toddler doesn't stop their bad behavior. However, as a discipline strategy, over-talking is just as bad as becoming overly emotional.

While your toddler lacks the cognitive ability to understand your very complex sentences, your two- to three-year-old still lacks the attention span even if they have the language skills. Instead of speaking in long, complex sentences, communicate in short phrases, restating them a couple of times, and incorporating inflections in your tone and your facial expressions.

For example, if your toddler gives you a good swat to the knee, say, "No, Julie! Don't hit Mommy/Daddy! That hurts. No hitting. No hitting." As they get older, say around three, you can start incorporating the consequences into the sentence, but keep it simple the younger they are.

#6 Give Time-Outs

Time-outs should be used when repeated redirections, reprimands, and loss of privileges don't cure your toddler's negative behavior. Time-outs are one of the best discipline methods for children this age, but before you impose the time-out, make sure to put on your serious face and give a warning in a stern voice. If your toddler doesn't listen during the countdown of three to one, then it's time to go to the time-out room or chair.

Remember, make sure not to talk to your toddler during this time. This is their time to reflect on what they did wrong. When the time-out is over, you can ask them to apologize to you, and when they do, give them a big hug to let them know you're no longer angry with them. Toddlers don't like to be separated from their parents and toys, so time-outs tend to work really well at this age. Enjoy them while they work!

#7 Stay Positive

No matter how frustrating your toddler's behavior is, don't vent about their bad behavior in front of them. If you heard your boss say something really negative about you at work, then you'd lose respect for your boss. It's the same thing when your toddler hears you talking about them in a negative or hopeless way. If they don't have a good image of you as the boss, then they end up repeating their negative behavior.

Still, it's normal to feel exasperated. In fact, if you don't feel exasperated from time to time, then your toddler is an alien. On a more serious note, you should turn to a friend, pediatrician, or a spouse for support and advice when you feel overwhelmed.

In this next section, we'll look at the appropriate tactics for the different age stages of toddlers.

Appropriate Discipline for Different Ages

Disciplining your child effectively will all depend on what age range your toddler falls into. Let's take a look at the guides for eighteen months, two years, and three years to figure out how you should be disciplining your child.

Eighteen Months

At this age, your child is fearless, mobile, curious, impulsive, and clueless about all the consequences of their actions, which is definitely a recipe for trouble. They're exercising independence while still needing reassurance at the same time, which is a tricky equilibrium to maintain. It's a lot like this. Your eighteen-month-old baby is running down the hall away from you, but he or she is still looking over their shoulder to make sure you're there if they need you.

While your toddler is building vocabulary at this stage and is able to follow the simplest of instructions, they cannot effectively communicate what they want and cannot understand your lengthy reprimands. Your toddler might bite or hit to get your attention or to let you know they're upset. Consequences of misbehaving at this age have to be immediate. Waiting just five minutes to react to what happened will confuse your toddler because they won't understand why you're reprimanding them. They won't tie the consequence to the action.

Two Years

At this age, your toddler is using their growing motor skills to test the limits by jumping, running, throwing, and climbing things. They're speaking a few words right now, and become frustrated when they can't get their point across to you. This is the age where they're prone to tantrums. Your toddler is self-centered at this stage and doesn't like to share.

People tend to call this stage the terrible twos, but it's really more like the autonomous twos. Consequences during this age must be swift because your toddler does not have a sense of time yet. Since they still lack impulse control, give them another chance soon after the incident has occurred.

Three Years

Your toddler has now become very talkative and uses language to argue their point of view. They love to be around other children, and a have a lot of energy, so they have a hard time playing quietly at home at this age. Taking your three-year-old to karate classes, dance classes, or to the gym gives them the social interaction they're craving, and allows them to release that excess energy.

At this age, your toddler needs interaction with other children as much as they need affection from you and food. It is not a want, but a necessity. Your toddler knows right from wrong at this stage, understands actions and consequences, and retains information for many hours. Consequences can be delayed to get the maximum impact, and explanations can contain more detail. For example, if your toddler throws cereal at you, remind your toddler about the no-food-throwing rule, and then explain that if he does this again, he won't get to watch his favorite show. When he asks to watch television, let him or her know that they cannot because they threw food earlier today.

Chapter 16: More Tips In Raising Your Daughter Well

In raising your daughter, there are a lot of things to consider that could affect her future life. Things like education, her environment and the habits she develops will affect how she will live in the long run; that's why it's necessary for you to understand the importance and relevance of these things to her well-being.

As a parent of a girl, you have to make allowances and provide extra space for your daughter to grow. Research has proven that what is important in helping your daughter grow from the inside out is to give her guidance, while at the same time letting her make her own mistakes and letting her learn from them.

**As she grows into adolescence, she will want to spend less time with you and more time outside with her friends more often than not. This is something that all parents will go through, and something that you should not be upset about. Teenagers naturally seek independence from their parents and wish to prove their adulthood to the people around her.

**Though it is not always possible to be friends with your daughter, building bridges is important. Parents usually fail to get closer to their daughters due to the fact that they have to maintain parental authority. However, studies have proven that doing fun activities with your daughter will not only strengthen your relationship with her but will also bring her closer to the family and further from danger.

**If your daughter comes to you and asks for permission to go to a party, instead of saying no right away, ask her questions and details about the event, where it's happening and who is going to host it. Give your daughter valid reasons why she cannot go and let her argue why she should, even if you have decided that she is not allowed to go to the party. This same technique can be applied in many other situations.

**Set your daughter's allowance. Do not give her something for doing nothing. Before you give her money, think first of the things that she might spend on. Since on most occasions you buy her clothes, she will most likely just buy the extra ones she likes. Give them chores or something to do in return of receiving an allowance.

**Always open your communication with her for her safety. Every parent wants to keep their daughter safe. Investing on things such as a cellphone for your daughter will help you in keeping track of where she is or in keeping her in touch.

**Girls need boundaries. Most teens tell their parents that their friends do not have curfews, when in fact they do. Letting your daughter stay out for long hours can obviously be dangerous for her. Teenagers also need their sleep. Lacking basic needs such as sleep will lead to poor health and low grades. Though it is important to set a curfew, it's okay to give her some allowance and bit of flexibility.

**Psychologically, teenagers respond better to rewards than punishments. If you want your daughter to clean up her bedroom, offer a reward instead of a warning. Choose your words carefully.

**As what has been mentioned, communication is important. Parents will feel it when their daughter has a problem, and when she does, ask her what's wrong and be there to comfort her. If she is in no mood to tell you, it is important that you do not push her, but be a shoulder that she can cry on.

** Along with independence, it is also important that you let your daughter experience love. There will come a time when teenagers will seek romantic relationships with the opposite or same sex, and this is inevitable. During the relationship, stand by her side and be her support. Openness about topics such as sex should be encouraged as well. Studies have shown that talking less about sex will only make your daughter curious in trying it out. Mentioning pregnancy and safe sex should not freak you out, but of course do not talk about this while she is with friends.

** Menstruation will also come soon as she reaches adolescence; therefore, preparation for this is also important.

**Just the same as sex and pregnancy, talk to her about drugs, smoking and alcohol. Under any circumstance, drugs should not be allowed in the house, as these things are illegal. However, things like alcohol can be bought when she reaches the right age.

**Screaming at her to get her to do what you want will not work without her feeling bad. Instead of yelling at her when she has mood swings, let her sort out her emotions. These mood swings are results of hormonal changes that happen inside her body, and she has no control over them.

**You should also watch out for any negative comments against your daughter. Odd comments from her friends, enemies or her family members can easily affect her emotions. Try to notice any signs of bulimic traits, depression or anorexia for these may prove to be serious.

Chapter 17: Life Ahead For A Confident Girl

Raising a happy and confident child is one of the toughest jobs in the world yet it is also one of the most fulfilling and most rewarding. When done right at a young age, you are essentially opening up a world full of success and happiness for your daughter.

By nurturing your child's self-esteem as early as you can, at age 6 to 9 in particular, you are building a foundation strong enough to withstand the troubles and issues of the upcoming years. Taking your job as parents seriously paves the way to a happy and confident future where your child can freely pursue her dreams and achieve her full potential.

So even if the process of raising a child with high self-esteem is tricky and difficult, the payoff is all worth it considering the exciting benefits and promising life ahead for your daughter. Among the top benefits of a healthy self-esteem for young girls include the following:

A Healthy Sense of Beauty

Girls with high self-esteem are not going to be easily swayed in their belief of what real beauty is. When they hit their teen years, they are less likely to succumb to common problems among teens including eating disorders, bullying, depression and suicidal tendencies.

Superior Social Skills

High self-esteem is also your child's ticket to better social skills. When she feels good about herself, she will be more comfortable socializing with other people, making friends and keeping relationships healthy.

Academic Success

At a time when school is a huge part of what makes up your child's world, high self-esteem will allow her to excel in her academics. She'll feel even more proud of her achievements because she knows and sees that her efforts are paying off. Unlike other kids with low self-esteem, she'll have better focus on what's important and what's not.

Better Behavioral Choices

A girl who knows she is loved and valued often creates a teen who knows how to choose her behavioral tendencies better. She is less likely to be influenced by her peers. Although she'd still love to take risk and experiment, she knows her boundaries and limits. She is also less likely to rebel when she doesn't get what she wants and she'll know how to handle the major changes that will happen in the upcoming years ahead.

Established Values and Character

Though self-esteem fluctuates through the years, nurturing it early allows your child to have an established set of values that will serve as her moral compass as she continues to grow up. Self-esteem if strong enough can hone her character to be a better teen and a better adult eventually.

Chapter 18: Modern Children And Religion

Even before now, the religion of a man has always been a touchy subject to discuss. This is because the matters of religion have never been just about who or what a man calls God. It is far deeper than that. It is the core beliefs of a man, it is the essential part of what makes a man who he is. The religion of a parent more often than not overflows and becomes the religion that the child will also practice. However, there is always the possibility that the child will decide to go their own way and practice a different religion. I don't think this should bother you as a parent; what you should be concerned about as a parent are the values and beliefs that whatever religion your child chooses to practice teaches him/her, even if it is the religion that you practice too.

There are so many religions in this world, and while many of the ways the religions are practiced, their beliefs about God or their gods vary very widely. From the studies of many religious scholars, there are a few things that are common to most, if not all religions. These are the fact that they all preach love for the next person, they teach kindness as their core value, many of them have their basis in terms of discipline and commitment. Most religions also offer us a way to see the value in our lives that ascends the trivial ways of our daily activities.

It is, therefore, your duty as a parent to teach your kids all the values which your religion teaches and your personal beliefs. Also, you should let them be aware of the other religions and let them be able to shape their opinions about them, because in the end, no one person can actually dictate what religion or what God a person should serve.

Here are some paragraphs from sacred books of different religions and their take on children.

For instance, in **Islam** , it is believed that once a child is conceived, it has the right to life. According to the Quran, all life is sacred. It is therefore not permissible to terminate a pregnancy because a person is maybe afraid of what taking care of the child might mean for the parent or the child. However, it is believed that God is the provider and sustainer of life.

"...Kill not your children because of poverty- We provide sustenance for you and for them." (Quran 6:151)

In **Christianity** too, here are some quotes about children.

"Train up a child in the way he should go; even when he is old he will not depart from it." (Proverbs 22:6)

"So, whatever you wish that others would do to you, do also to them, for this is the law and the prophets." (Matthew 7:12)

In **Buddhism,** we have quotes like this.

Here is one of Buddha's quotes on authenticity.

"However, many holy words you read, however many you speak, what good will they do you if you do not act on upon them?"

This is something right here telling you to act as you would like to see your children act.

"The heart is like a garden. It can grow compassion or fear, resentment or love, what seeds will you plant there?"

This is also another quote talking about what we teach our children. The kind of values we imbibe in them would determine the kind of person they grow up to be.

In **Yoruba Ifa Religion**, there are quotes like:

"Regard heaven as your father, earth as your mother and all that lives as your brother and sister."

This was meant to teach the concept of respect for our parents and love for our neighbors.

"If a man sees a snake and a woman kills it, all that matters is that it does not escape."

This is a quote to teach responsibility.

All of these quotes just go on to show that regardless of what religion it is that you practice, the core values of religion in itself are what matter the most. This is what you should teach to your kids and you can be reassured that in the end, when your child chooses your religion or doesn't, you will be sure that it is for the right reasons.

Chapter 19: Coping With Long-Distance Parenting

FREQUENT COMMUNICATION

You are missing your child and him or she must be missing you too. So, if you can afford it, try to communicate on a daily basis, and then figure out a reasonable amount of time you can spend on the phone each time you call. Some parents may be busier than others, so the frequency of your communication with your children and the people taking care of them would determine the relationship between you and them. As a matter of fact, do not let any vacuum exist between you and your children because if you allow that to happen, filling it might be much more difficult.

There is not set magical amount of time that parents should spend on phone or the Internet, it all depends on the availability of time and schedule should be based on that. In fact, if you spend couple of minutes or hour communicating with your kid or kids that would be ideal. Sometimes, only daily 20 minutes or sometimes even just a call to say "goodnight," would be fine.

Factually, communicating effectively with one's child from wherever you may be is perhaps one of the toughest challenges that parents have to face. However, in spite of trying to open a two-way communication line with our children, it gets frustrating if we find that their attention is not on the ongoing conversation or on us at all. At times, parents complain about broken communication lines between them and the kids. But when tried to communicate with the children all the time, we find it completely alright to converse with them even when we are folding clothes, reading the newspaper, writing letters or cooking meals.

As we all know, naturally children get easily distracted and do not always respond as expected of them to what goes on around them most of the time. It becomes the duty of the parents to encourage positive communication patterns and attitude by endeavoring efforts towards discouraging them from the act of ignorance in communication.

However, in order to make sure that an acceptable agreement is reach, parents themselves must listen to whatever the child wants to contribute during the conversation. It is very important for parents to educate their children on proper communication format.

TECHNOLOGICAL EXPOSURE

To enhance their knowledge in modern technological innovations, it is the duty of parents to expose them to the use of some communication gadgets. Teaching by example is the best method every parent must practice in order to give adequate attention to the children.

Obviously, while conversing with your children, you must direct your complete attention on them and total focus on the conversation. You may allow voicemail to take your in-coming calls, turn the television off or even go to a room with no distractions if that is what it takes to get the kids attention too. Whenever necessary, you must gently and in age appropriate terms explain to your children what is wrong with their form of communication. Because in distance parenting, any time you spend talking to your child is worth the trouble.

Noticeably, kids are after all kids and it is normal for them to be non-communicative and non-reactive sometimes. The children are your domain and consequently, you should know best how to interpret their behaviors and gauge areas of improvement in their communication skills. Teaching your children positive communication skills is the best way of ensuring that they imbibe healthy communication patterns in their daily lives.

FREQUENT VISITATION

Try to visit your kids very often and that will rekindle your parental relationship with him or her. In fact, always set a date in advance and whenever you want to adjust your timetable, you let them know. Planning for a visit gives you and your family at home something to look forward to.

Visits can be such a wonderful interaction between parents and the kids left behind in a distance away. It is always better to plan a trip in advance and save up money towards the visit. Whatever it takes, always know that it is worth making the trip to see the ones you love.

INTERNET AND WEBCAM

In the past, it was not an easy or cheap task to call home frequently just to ask how the children were faring at home. But in today's world, because of the Internet, there are a lot of ways to call your home without paying through your nose. Therefore, parents should call the house to inquire how the children are doing. Parents should call home from the office quite frequently, so that the person taking care of the kids while he, she or both aren't physically home. That will ginger the Caregiver or Nanny into more sincere and honest action towards the kids.

Try to have good Internet connection with reasonable speed that will enable you to see your children through a webcam. When you purchase a good webcam, Skype is easily downloadable and you could start using it straightaway. You can start with the free version of Skype if you can't afford the paid version.

A webcam allows more interaction than a phone ever could. A webcam gives you the ability to learn your children body language and facial expressions. Interactions are also much more enjoyable and there is less pressure to speak when you don't have much to say. There is a big advantage of using a webcam versus using the phone alone.

PRESENCE SIMULATION

It is extremely essential for parents who leave the care of their kids to other people to simulate their presence with the children quite often. The parents could do that by creating time to be with them online, chatting or on the phone, talking.

During such times, important activities in their lives should be topic for discussion, such as: about school work, if everything is fine in school and at home, household chores, social activities, school home work, and many other things surrounding their daily lives.

In fact, you can even make some of your routines together, like singing songs together and telling them to sleep when it is time to go to bed. You can even use the time to talk about family matters if the child is old enough to understand and give suggestions. Parents should discuss things going on in their child's life.

Although, it would be a bit expensive to be on the phone for a long time, but at the long run, it would worth the monetary sacrifice. Nowadays, with the modern day communication technology, the cost might be minimal when compared to the risk of not monitoring the affairs of your children closely.

How often are you fully and completely present when you are with your children? One of the greatest gifts we can give to our children is to be fully present with them. I know, this can often be a big challenge to most of us in the current shift of the paradigm in the global economy.

When my three children were growing up, I worked for many years full time as an OFW and that was when I started making notes about this book. I traveled back to the Philippines to see my kids and handled my commitments and in addition to spending time with my husband.

Obviously, that was the only period I could be fully present with the kids.

However, when I was with my children during the vacation, I always set aside "time alone" with them. "Time alone" was daily quality time I spent with each of my children, doing whatever they wanted to do. During this time I did not answer the phone or deal with the many issues of running a household. It was time set aside to be fully present with them, not even thinking about other things.

The message you give to your children when you don't spend quality time being fully present is that they are not important. When answering the phone, or getting things done, or thinking about what you have to do tomorrow is more important than being present with your children, they get the message that being with them and really knowing them is not very important to you.

When I was growing up, my parents were always busy in the farm. They never had the time to just be with me and my siblings. Even in the Evening when they came back from the farm the never wanted to know about our thoughts and feelings, or about how things were going on at school. They never had the time to play with us or just hang out with me and my siblings. Although, while they said that they loved us occasionally and that we were important to them, I never felt it. Words don't cut it when the actions don't follow to complement it.

If it is not important to you to just be with your children, talking with them, playing with them, taking a walk, holding them, listening to them, sharing love with them, gazing at them with love, then they will likely not feel loved by you. No matter how many things you buy them, or how often you tell them you love them, if they are not important enough to you to really be with them, then it is likely they will not feel loved and cherished by you.

Our children need our focused attention, and when they don't get it, they may pull for it in various ways. They may talk on and on, trying to draw closer attention. They may act out by fighting with each other, or by not listening to you or going into resistance regarding chores, homework, hygiene, bedtime, and so on. For many children, even negative attention feels better than no attention at all. This may create a very negative vicious circle within your relationship with them. In that case, the more they act out, the less you are feeling like being with them, but the less you are with them in a loving and attentive way and the more they may act out.

Think about how you feel when someone gives you his or her full attention. Doesn't it feel wonderfully well? How often does someone look you in the eyes and give you his or her full attention? How often do you feel really listened to and heard by someone? Unfortunately, many people are so intent on being listened to and heard that they don't listen and hear others.

The simple act of being fully present with your children will do more for them than you can imagine. I have now taken my family with me and many friends of mine who were deeply impacted by a friend or relative, who really listened to them, even if it only occurred occasionally, can tell the difference.

You have an opportunity to give your children a great gift of being fully present with them, with your love, compassion, empathy, interest, sense of humor, playfulness, and affection. You have the opportunity even if it is just for half an hour, to fully cherish your kids. They grow up so fast. Don't miss this opportunity of getting bonded with them each day and anytime.

COMPLIMENT YOUR KIDS

Always remember to compliment your child for a job well done whenever there is a need for praise. Commend the good traits they naturally possess, and suggest ways that will help them learn from their mistakes and failures. Of course, parents should give praise when it is due to their children. But encouragement does not thrive on praises alone. In fact, children can differentiate empty praises from real ones. Besides, there is danger that a child hungry for praise will merely conform just to please the parent and won't feel okay unless he or she gets praised. Encouragement means emphasis on strengths and assets, other than faults. It is non-judgmental to accept the level of accomplishment of each child.

It is very important for a child's healthy development to reasonably, feel important and worthy. Healthy self-esteem is a child's armor against the challenges of the world. As a matter of fact, children who feel good of themselves seem to have an easier time handling conflicts and resist negative pressures much easier.

Obviously, unrealistic expectations by parents could be stressful to a child, especially if circumstances or physical inability prevents him or her from fulfilling certain expectations. The kid would be bound for certain disappointment. It's just like saying "It won't hurt" when an injection really hurts. In this modern time, parents can't fool children all the time.

Sometimes, the parents have to help the children set realistic goals. When one of the kids wants to enter a contest, you're all out rooting for him or her, whether it's an art contest, a science contest, or whatever. Some kids start counting their prizes even before they submit their entries. In those cases, you explain the odds and make the project so much fun that it is the effort that counts.

Certainly, when parents compliment their children, they tend to smile more readily and feel more contented and enjoy a better life. And realistically, kids are more optimistic about life when complimented by their parents quite often. Study has shown that children who feel important are well-rounded, respectful, and excel in academics, in extracurricular activities and hobbies and able to develop healthier relationships with others.

Our children need to be a part of our life, not our whole life. We need to role-model for them what it looks like to take personal responsibility for filling ourselves up. We need to show them what it looks like to take responsibility for making ourselves happy, rather than rely on them for our happiness. Your children want to know that they are important to you, but not so important that your well-being is dependent upon them.

If this is what you are doing, it is not good for your children. It is a huge burden on children to be responsible for their parent's loneliness and sense of purpose. Children who feel this responsibility often become caretakers, giving themselves up to take care of a parent. On the other hand, a child burdened with this responsibility may rebel and distance from the parent, spending less and less time at home to avoid the burden of the parent's emptiness.

Chapter 20: Give them time

Give them time. This is probably the hardest part. Give them time that they may need to solve issues. Give them space to solve their own issues. Trust them to come to you if it's something they need or want advice or help on. The basis of trust has been laid, lines of communication have been opened, and now it's time to trust that your child is kind and trusting enough to let you know when they need you. That you've instilled the trust that you will always be there when it matters.

This should be all that I have to say about this, but I actually have a story to share. My oldest, a twelve-year-old girl, struggled with bullies at school for a long time. She tried in vain to handle it on her own, but was repeatedly unsuccessful. She went to the office to fill out paperwork, but like most schools, time to deal with issues like this is sparse from the administration.

I could see this weighing on her, but she wasn't ready to talk about it. It hurt to watch her suffer in silence every day, but she wasn't ready to talk. I stayed open, waited for her to be ready. She exhausted avenue after avenue, trying to solve the problem without getting me involved. When she finally got the nerve up to tell me, I was bursting with pride. It hadn't worked, but she had been willing to try to solve her own problem on her own. Interpersonal relationships aren't always easy, and she understood that, and she tried to reach out an olive branch. The branch was rejected, so she went to her instructor. The instructor couldn't do much but attempt to mediate between the pair. None of this seemed to work, so she finally came to me, spoke to me, and we talked about people and about how she could only control her own reaction to the situation. We talked about severity, and while we did involve the principal to offer a solution, and I was proud to say that my child took to high road, even if it was unpopular. We discussed what doing the right thing really mean, at least in the long run, and whether it would make her popular enough.

She thanked me that day, happy to see that I didn't just spout a bunch of ideology at her, but showed her that being positive about life and problem solving wasn't always going to be an easy feat. That there were going to be struggles, but she tried to solve it, she tried to be the bigger person and when she needed me, I was there. While we did end up getting the school board involved, my child handled the entire ordeal with the kind of grace I rarely even see in adults.

Time wasn't an easy thing to give to my child. Honestly, it was frustrating to watch her suffer and not ready to talk to me, but I knew the truth. If I pushed her to talk, she very well may have closed off to me, problems with friends aren't always easy to discuss, especially with parents who's first instinct is to protect their child at all costs, often with little care to how the child wants to handle it. So I sat on my hands, and I waited, and it paid off.

I could have dug into her private journal, pried into her private thoughts, sat her down and told her that she had no choice but to speak to me, but she's nearly a teenager, and she has to learn how to become a young adult.

I gave her time and I gave her space. I trusted her to make the right choices in life, because I know the beautiful child that I raised, and I have faith in her, and she didn't let me down one bit. She is a creature of grace and strength, and after that time, I am always the first one to hear of any problems at school. Sometimes she comes to me and tells me that she doesn't want advice or help, but that she just wants someone to listen to her while she expresses her feelings about an event. Those are the moments that I just sit and listen, and no matter how much I want to interfere, as long as I don't feel that she's in any real danger or the situation has spiraled out of her control, I let her form her own plans to handle the problem, and because, she knows that I trust her to make the right choice she knows that she can come to me when she doesn't know what the right choice is.

And when she does, there are times that I don't know what the right choice is either, and in those moments, we discuss options, weigh the good and the bad of each decision and she picks the one that she thinks is the best one. Very rarely do I think it's the best way to handle things, but she's not me. She can't solve her problems the same way I do.

I know my children are good kids, and trust them to be able to speak to me when they have a problem and to be able to solve a lot of little issues on their own. If they spill something, it isn't the end of the world. Mistakes happen, and instead of either ignoring it or getting upset, they just clean it up and move on with their lives. It is in moments like this that I feel the kind of pride that comes from raising responsible positive kids that can handle the real world.

Love, trust and positivity aren't ever going to be completely easy and hiccup free in this world. It's always going to take a lot of work and energy. But in the end, I've found that the results were worth it, children that not only remain positive, but have learned that the world is something they can change only by changing themselves, becoming a great example to others and being a good person who can handle whatever life throws at them. As a parent, my goal is to be able to send my child out into the world, well equipped to handle any sort of challenges that life sends their way. They're beautiful little people that deserve nothing better than the best, but I know that even if the best doesn't come their way, they'll make the best out of whatever does. Those are the kinds of children I feel should be presented to the world, the children that can handle the good and the bad with grace and strength, that have confidence in themselves and the home that they always have open to come to. Children that aren't afraid of the world, and don't let it bowl down their beauty into some shell of what it once was. Positive parenting isn't always positive, but it helps create positive and healthy adults that make choices that lead them to more positive lives.

Children hold the future of the world in their hands, and those small hands will someday have to pass it on to the next generation, teaching them how to maintain their positivity in a sometimes terrifying world should be the biggest concern of every parent out there today, at least in my humble opinion.

Chapter 21: Where The Baby Should Sleep And Eat In An Rv

Traveling is one of world's favorite past times, no matter where you are. If you have a young baby, travel can be difficult, but manageable. However, there is one problem that every family faces when they have a baby and this is; where should the baby sleep and eat in an RV?

Having a baby does not mean that life has to stop or that you cannot travel. You can still travel, you just have to plan better and make certain accommodations that you normally would not have to – such as taking driving breaks while baby sleeps or making extra rest stops for those diaper changes and extra meals that babies need in order to sustain their energy to scream at you from the backseat.

No matter what country you are in, it is important to follow certain safety regulations and laws regarding where your baby sleeps and eats while you travel. When you have an RV, it may be tempting to allow your baby to sleep and eat in the living quarters while you are driving. However, in many countries this is illegal and in countries where it is not illegal, it is still unsafe.

So what accommodations must be made in order to ensure that your baby's needs are met, but you can still travel in style with your family and friends?

Never Advertise "Baby On Board"

While these signs are cute and you think you are protecting your child from unsafe drivers, you are actually making yourself a target at rest stops and gas stations. You are inviting kidnappers to invade your space and risking the safety of your child at every stop you make – and with a baby, you will be making a lot of stops.

Prepare For All Types of Weather

If you are traveling a long distance, you do not know what the temperature, or the weather are going to be like while you are traveling. For your baby's sake, prepare for all types of weather that can be expected for the season and check the weather patterns online before leaving for your destination.

Safety Concerns With Eating and Sleeping

When the RV is in motion, your baby should be in a car seat at all times. They should never be allowed either attended or unattended in the living quarters of the vehicle. If there were an accident, the baby could be tossed through the cabin, and seriously harmed.

You should never feed the baby while the RV is moving. This is because a sudden jolt or need to slam on the breaks could cause the baby to choke on their food – whether it is formula, breast milk, or solid food.

Essentially, if the RV is moving, the baby should be secured in their car seat at all times.

When you are sleeping as a family, always ensure that the doors to your RV are locked. This is not just for your safety; it is for the safety of your baby as well. Each year, hundreds of babies are reported missing from rest stops. The main reason is that the parents failed to lock the doors.

Where Should Baby Sleep and Eat?

Your baby should only sleep in their car seat as long as the vehicle is still in motion. The baby should only eat if the vehicle is in the parked position. This may mean that it takes longer to make it to your destination, but your baby's health and well-being takes precedence when it comes to traveling.

Plan for Extra Pit Stops

If you are taking a road trip with a baby that must eat or sleep on a certain schedule, make sure to plan their schedule into your itinerary. Choose pit stops along the way that allow for your baby's naps. While your baby is napping it is a great time to refresh yourself for the road and stretch your legs. You may even want to take a nap while your baby is sleeping as well. This will help counteract the time necessary for your baby to sleep well, and to prevent exhaustion while you are on the road.

Planning Around Meals

Planning around meals and snacks can be difficult. For meals, most families pull over to eat and enjoy a meal together. However, snacks may be a different story but they must be accommodated in order to make the baby happy and ensure that they get proper nutrition. There are products on the market that are meant for babies who are traveling. They are snacks that dissolve in the baby's mouth to prevent choking so that there is no risk of choking while you are traveling.

Choose Your Destinations Wisely

When you are traveling with a little one, it is important that you take the time to plan trips that are kid friendly. For example, you do not want to plan a trip to Las Vegas to gamble while you have a six month old in tow. You will want to choose family friendly destinations that involve short trips and choose roads that have the advantage of pit stops on a regular basis to ensure that your baby's needs can be met.

Start with shorter trips and slowly work your way up to longer trips to allow your baby to become accustomed to the idea of traveling in the RV. If your baby is older, and used to being in the car seat, you may not have as much of a problem. But babies who are still in a car seat that lays down can become sore very easily from riding for long periods of time when they are not used to it. This can make for a very grumpy baby by the end of the trip. Make sure to add extra padding to the car seat to help ensure that your baby is comfortable and does not develop sore spots on his back and bottom.

Chapter 22: Friends & Siblings

Can small children be friends? They can but in their own way. That means you should be prepared to see one bite the other, take the toy without asking ... These are things of the age that need to be understood. In the range of 1 to 3 years, the child is still egocentric, and the question of the possession of objects is very present. Therefore, it is common for them to take a toy from the other's hand and walk.

The little ones are in the famous oral phase, in which they use the mouth as a means of discovering the world. As long as they do not know how to talk, they end up sometimes hitting for no reason, just to get what they want. Of course, if aggressive behavior is too frequent and intense, it requires parental attention. It is not necessary to deprive the one who was caught up in the other's life but to ensure that it happens in the most protected way possible, supervising and separating in case of aggression.

Not infrequently, a more passive child becomes friends with a bossy one. The experts consulted say that the leaderships of the group begin to dawn with 4 or 5 years. When this happens, others become his followers - and make no mistake about their little age: the leader realizes the strength his opinion has over others.

When the teacher identifies this in school, he should use strategies and jokes to dilute this configuration so that roles are reversed in some situations: followers become leaders, and the leader becomes a follower - this can also be done at home by parents. If conflicts arise from the relationship between a leader and a follower, it is recommended that each child should orally expose the other to how he felt and what he did not like. They should listen and try to resolve the situation with each other.

Shy Children

More introverted and shy children may have difficulty making friends. In such cases, parents may approach a class in the playground of the building, for example, and introduce the child, asking if he can play with them. So, next time, he will already have a reference on how to act. You can also invite classmates to attend your home. That way, they will have what to talk about in the room, plus memories of fun times together.

But if the child is never called to any party and seems to be always isolated, the ideal is to do a job with the school to detect why this happens. You can also enroll your child in extracurricular theatre or sports classes that help decrease inhibition. Just do not press it.

If your child is very sociable and makes friends easily, rest easy. Just be aware of whether your child is not acting that way to get attention and can do a little more work with a concentration in the classroom. Point it out that there is time for everything.

Friends – Siblings

Who said siblings could not be good friends? In these cases, one only needs attention if the youngest becomes a" shadow "of the brother and ends up having no personality. Well, then, talk about the importance of having your own attitudes.

There are also cases where siblings have no affinity. Parents should be aware of the context in which the lack of friendship happens and the expectation they have of that relationship. In general, siblings will be friends but often go through situations of jealousy and competition. It may also be that they have different interests, which seems like a lack of friendship, but is related to gender and age. Parents need to look at how they relate to the family (mother, father, and siblings) in order to identify whether they have a strong or superficial bond because the child perceives and tends to have similar behaviors.

Leaving

If the parents look back, they'll remember that some of their own friends walked away for a while and then came back. You have to stay calm and keep in mind that this is a process of building the bond of the child. Another feeling that can arise in such a situation is jealousy. When there is some dependence on friendship, attention is needed. If we identify something negative, that does not benefit both parties. It is necessary to stimulate new friends. The adult should show that the child can discover affinities with several children.

Outside The Party

Make no mistake, this will happen sooner or later, either for financial reasons (it's expensive to invite all the students) or affinity. In these situations, the adult needs to be prepared to face the frustration - of the child and parent. Parents must accept that it is not the end of the world and explain that some people identify more with each other than with others.

The opportunity is ideal for sitting with the child and asking why he thought he was so close to the birthday boy. Sometimes he thinks he's friends with the other, but he's not reciprocated. It is important to have this understanding, that some people give the impression that they are our friends, but they are not.

Conclusion

Thank you again for downloading this book!

I hope you were able to get reassuring answers to your nagging questions and concerns about single fatherhood from this book.

The next step is to transform all the encouragement and advice in this book into a plan of action that will help you overcome all the challenges of single parenting and emerge a victorious and proud single dad.

Thank you and good luck!

www.ingramcontent.com/pod-product-compliance
Lightning Source LLC
Chambersburg PA
CBHW072008070526
44583CB00015B/1387